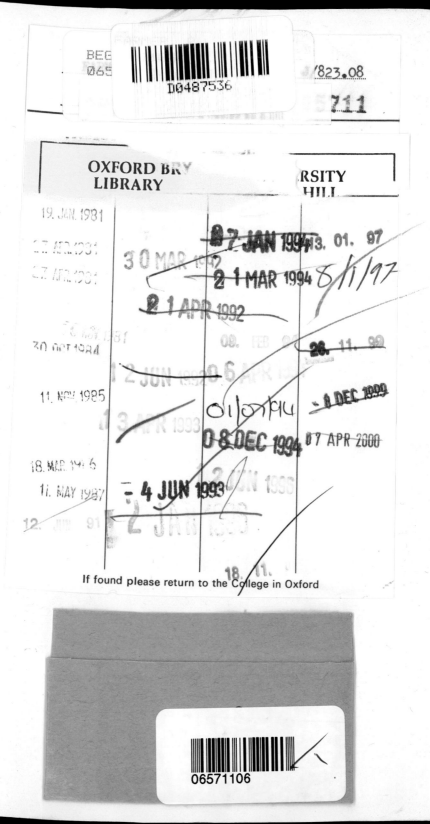

BEGINNINGS

Creation Myths of the World

BEGINNINGS

Creation Myths of the World
Compiled and edited by
Penelope Farmer
and illustrated by
Antonio Frasconi

1978 · CHATTO & WINDUS · LONDON

Published by
Chatto & Windus Ltd.,
40–42 William IV Street,
London WC2N 4DF

Clarke, Irwin & Co. Ltd.,
Toronto

The Editor acknowledges the assistance of the Arts Council of Great Britain in preparing this book.

British Library Cataloguing in Publication Data
Beginnings: creation myths of the world.
1. Creation - Juvenile Literature
I. Farmer, Penelope
291.1′3   BL325C7
ISBN 0-7011-2275-7

Printed in Great Britain by
R. & R. Clark Ltd, Edinburgh

Contents

for

Margaret McElderry

In my beginning is my end . . .
. . . In my end is my beginning.

T. S. Eliot

I saw no way – the Heavens were stitched –
I felt the columns close –
The earth reversed her Hemispheres –
I touched the Universe – . . .

Emily Dickinson

THE BEGINNING AND THE END

'*I am lonely, I want to make a world*' *cries Bhagavan, one creator god. And that is it, precisely – for we are all lonely, have always been since the beginning of time, have tried each of us to make ourselves a world, quick, quick, before the great black hole that is the universe sucks us in entirely. Hence creation myths. Because to tell how the world began, how we came by fire – and food – and death – even to hazard guesses at how it might all end – is in a sense to recreate it for ourselves; so to make ourselves less lonely perhaps, and so counter a little the remoteness and indifference of the stars.*

This was not of course the mythmakers' conscious intention, even where their stories were a serious attempt to explain the world about them; (for many others do seem decidedly tongue-in-cheek, like the one where an Indian Adam and Eve have to be taught to make – and drink – rice wine before they understand how to reproduce themselves, no serpent being available, or where another god took a rest before he set about creating the English – to take but two examples). Perhaps only those stories used in religious life and ritual were ever meant to be believed implicitly, as the biblical creation myth still is in certain quarters. Yet even so none need be dismissed as charming but infantile fantasies the way they used to be by some early ethnologists, working at a time when the world seemed more secure and science, underpinned by a little discreet religion, able potentially to offer explanations for everything. We know that not all truth is factual or ever will be. No matter how much we may think we ought by now to discard the less rational answers, we cannot quite manage to, bound willingly or unwillingly to the other kinds of truth these stories breathe, in their differences as in their astonishing likenesses. (Why, for instance, should that myth of earth emerging from a giant egg crop up in places as far apart as Polynesia, Africa and Finland, but not that I can discover in the Americas?) It is a curious phenomenon altogether, myth, tough as leather, fragile as glass – hardly a story bears logical analysis; cannot be shattered by a blow from a sharp mind; yet the very next minute is whole again. In some weird way the illogic of myth has even

The Beginning and the End   3

succeeded in anticipating science. In it you can find prefigured the big bang theory of the origin of earth (Hawaii); the expanding universe (Navaho Indian); the origin of life in stagnant water (Dahomey, West Africa). At whatever level you look at it, for whatever reason, psychic, symbolic, scientific – even simply for amusement – if you gaze long enough you may find myth beginning to explode whole systems and reconstructing them for you. After making this collection I doubt if my thinking will ever be quite the same again.

In particular, taken as a whole, these myths have seemed to me to point quite distinctly – yet without ever directly expressing it – to some kind of unity behind creation, not a static unity, but a forever shifting breathing one, forever seemingly disunited, then unified again; something I now know relates well enough to the discovery by modern nuclear physicists that matter and space alike are composed of the same varieties of infinitesimal particles in ever-shifting combinations. Moreover the movement of these particles in their turn, forever colliding with one another, forever being destroyed and forever in their very destruction recreated, reflects the more explicit message of the myths, that in order to create something has to be destroyed. The earth, for instance, is made from the body of a giant or dragon; has to be renewed by destruction in fire or flood; will only grow food plants from the blood or flesh of some slain god, while the acquisition by man of life or food or fire has to be paid for by the acceptance of death – the message is everywhere, quite unmistakable. To live is to die; to die is to live. 'In my beginning is my end' . . . 'In my end is my beginning' said T. S. Eliot. But the mythmakers arrived there long before he did.

EARTH

In the beginning was the word . . .

St. John's Gospel

Where wast thou when I laid the foundations of the earth? Declare, if thou hast understanding. Who determined the measures thereof, if thou knowest? Or who stretched the line upon it . . . or who laid the corner stone thereof; when the morning stars sang together, and all the sons of God shouted for joy . . .?

The Book of Job

In so many languages the word earth names not only the soil beneath our feet but also our planet. We are, literally, rooted in it. And in most cultures too (one important exception the Egyptian) the myth-makers, while regarding the sky as male, have called the earth female; that is the one who gives birth. And have then asked: who gave it birth? How did it begin? Their answers, given particular local detail, reflect very well the extraordinary way in which the same mythical thinking recurs over and over again in every corner of the world. Mythologists, anthropologists, ethnologists, psychologists have suggested historical, geographical, psychological, even neurological causes for this. To which I can add nothing, except to say that I do not for one moment believe it is all simple coincidence.

There are four main themes to these answers. Earth is made from the body of some monster/god/giant – as in the earliest known creation myth of all, the Babylonian, dating from the twelfth century BC. *Or it emerges from some giant egg or other kind of shell. Or it evolves from a void, either spontaneously as in the Hawaiian version or because it is ordered to (. . . 'Let there be light' . . .). Or it is formed as by a weaver or a carpenter or a potter, sometimes with assistance from the devil in those parts of the world where the devil figures. In many stories more than one theme occurs, and all four are more or less universal, even if absent in some specific areas (apart from failing to find an egg in the Americas I have so far failed to track down a giant in Africa).*

Yet of all the ideas they contain, the most striking, for me, is the one Christians have tended, wrongly, to appropriate as if unique to themselves, the idea of word as first principle. There are three other examples here, Mayan, Maori and Tanzanian; the Gospel of St. John could only possibly have influenced the Mayan myth and I doubt even that. It is a fundamental perception in any event and perfectly logical as well as mystical. What distinguishes man from animals is precisely his ability to name things. There is a sense in which you could well say that something does not begin to exist until it has been named, until there is a word for it; not least the earth on which we stand.

¶ ... Before sky was; before earth was; before the gods were born; before there was any death ...

EGYPTIAN

¶ When there was neither heaven nor earth sounded the first word of God. And he unloosed Himself from His stone and declared His divinity. And all the vastness of eternity shuddered. And His word was a measure of grace and He broke and pierced the backbone of mountains. Who was born there? Who? Father, Thou knowest: He who was tender in heaven came into Being.

CENTRAL AMERICA, Maya

¶ The sky was large and very clear. It was empty; there were no stars and no moon; only a tree stood in the air and there was wind. This tree fed on the atmosphere and ants lived on it. Wind, tree, ants and atmosphere were controlled by the power of the Word. But the Word was not something that could be seen. It was a force that enabled one thing to create another. ...

AFRICA, TANZANIA Wapangwa

At a time when the earth became hot
At the time when the heavens turned about
At the time when the sun was darkened
To cause the moon to shine
The time of the rise of the Pleiades,
The slime, this was the source of the earth
The source of the night that made night
The intense darkness, the deep darkness
Darkness of the sun, darkness of the night
Nothing but night.
The night gave birth. ...

HAWAII

¶ Everything was water, water as far as the eye could see. But above the water rose the tree Teri-Ramula. As time passed a worm was born in the tree and it began to eat the wood. The dust fell into the water, year after year, until slowly the world was formed.

And then at last the tree fell to the ground. The bark on the lower side of the trunk became the skin of the world; the bark on the other side became the skin of the sky. The trunk itself turned into rock. The branches became the hills.

INDIA *Hill Miri*

¶ In the beginning there was no earth, only marsh and water. It was a wasteland, no life in it, no place for life. Over it arched the sky where the supreme God, Olodumare, lived with the other gods. The gods came down sometimes to play in the wasteland, swinging across it on huge spiders' webs strung as if they were bridges, here and there. But without solid ground to live on there were no men at all. So one day Olodumare called the great God Obtala and said, 'You, Obtala, must create an earth.' And he took a snail shell filled with loose earth from between his thighs and gave it to Obtala, together with some pieces of iron, a cock, a pigeon and a hen with five toes. Obtala swung down to the marshland across the spiders' web bridges. He threw down the pieces of iron, strewed over them earth from the snail shell, then set on top of the earth the cock, the pigeon and the hen with five toes. Immediately in the manner of cocks, pigeons and hens they began to scratch. They scratched and scratched, they scratched and scratched. Little by little they spread the earth further, little by little the solid earth was formed.

Then the other gods came down to live there to keep Obtala company, Obtala the great god whom the supreme god, Olodumare, had sent to create this earth with the help of a cock and a pigeon and a five-toed hen.

NIGERIA *Yoruba*

¶ Once the earth was a tiny disc, only big enough for God and the devil to lie upon together, and everything else was sea. The devil did not care for this at all, he wanted to get rid of God and have the earth to himself. So he said to God, 'You look tired, why don't you lie down and sleep and I will keep watch?' God knew everything, he knew the devil's mind precisely. Nevertheless he lay down there and pretended to sleep. Then the devil crept up behind him, got hold of God's shoulders and tried to push him into the sea. But he could not; though he seemed to be on the brink of it the shore kept stretching on and on, the sea marched ever further away. That was the north. So then the devil got hold of God's shoulders and pushed him towards the south, and again it was in vain, again the shore expanded and try as he might he could not reach the sea. He tried pushing God to the east; the same; he tried pushing him to the west; the same again. Afterwards the earth reached as far as the eye could see, and that was the beginning of the world.

BULGARIA

Creation Hymn

¶ When on high there was no heaven and no earth and neither heaven nor earth were named; when there was only water, the sweet water Apsu and the salt water Tiamet; they mingled together, and over the aeons Tiamet gave birth to the the gods, one by one, the last of them Ea, son of Anu, master of the sky. And all these gods reigned over the abyss. But after a while they began to quarrel. They grew noisy, they leapt in the belly of Tiamet, they kept Apsu their father awake with their tumult till in the end he could bear it no more and determined to destroy them. Yet they were Tiamet's young, she was reluctant to undo her own creation. And when Ea, all-seeing, learned the father's plan, he spoke one gentle word, charming Apsu into sleep, then bound Apsu, slew him instead. Afterwards Ea in his turn begot himself a son. Marduk was this son. He was the hero, the leader; he had four ears so there was no limit to his hearing, when he opened his mouth the fire sprang out; he was perfect, and mighty, he was the highest of them all – Ea was well pleased with him. And Anu, Ea's father, made the winds to be Marduk's army, both vanguard and rearguard, to harass Tiamet and Tiamet's sons. For meanwhile, all the other gods had gone to Tiamet their mother. 'Hear us,' they said. 'Apsu, our father, was murdered and you did not stir. Now they bring the winds from all the four quarters to harry us. Wake, rise up, mother, destroy them for us, punish them as they deserve.'

Tiamet grew angry in her turn. She spawned a new brood, monsters this time, not gods; serpents with poisoned fangs, dragons with rending claws, lions, fierce rabid dogs, fish men and scorpion men, a storm that howled in the abyss. Yet she herself remained the most fiercesome of all monsters, she was the mightiest of dragons still. She prepared for battle. She raised the clumsy Kingu to be her captain, to be her leader in the war. Ea and Anu trembled when they saw Tiamet's army. Only Marduk would be strong enough to confront her now they thought. For Marduk exulted in his power. He did not fear anything. They raised a throne for him, they robed him in the mantle of a king. They gave him weapons and invincible armour. 'Now go,' they said. 'Slit Tiamet's belly, kill her, let her blood stream out to all the quarters of the world.'

First Marduk made himself a bow. In his other hand he took a mace and a net that he had woven, each of its corners upheld by a single wind. He raised up all the other winds to help him, the whirl-wind, the tempest and the hurricane, the warm wind and the cold one, the wind of four and the wind of seven, last of all the tornado that nothing can withstand. Then he mounted his chariot and set out to look for Tiamet in her lair in the abyss. Long before he saw her he could hear her, raging. 'Upstart,' she shrieked when he came in sight. Marduk called out, 'Leave your monstrous hoards now, ancient mother. Stand up before it, you and I will fight it out alone.' Tiamet shrieked again, with terror now. Her legs shook. Her tail trembled. But still she launched herself upon him, Marduk threw out his net to entangle her, the warm wind flew from behind him to beat upon her face and when she opened her mouth to engulf him it blew inside and raged within her belly, swelling it up to twice its usual size. So then Marduk took aim and shot an arrow from his bow, slitting her belly. Immediately she died. Whereupon Marduk threw her body down and stood over it triumphantly, straddling the abyss. All Tiamet's brood then turned to flee, but Marduk's forces engulfed and captured them, while Marduk raised his mace and smashed their mother's skull, the blood streaming out and flowing to the furthest corners of the world. He stood and pondered on her slaying for a while. At last he split her body like a pair of cockle-shells. One half he raised to make the arc of the sky, confining the waters so they could not escape. He set limits to the firmament, he made a dwelling-place there for the gods, he set the sun and the moon in the heavens and defined their going and their coming.

From the other half of Tiamet's body Marduk made the earth. Her head was a mountain. Her breasts were the rich hills. He let great rivers, the Tigris and the Euphrates, flow from her eyes, but her nostrils he stopped up, hiding their waters deep within. He lifted up her tail to join the sky to earth, he set her back to hold the heavens in their place. And at last when all was done he made temples on the earth and consecrated them to his father Ea. Then Marduk washed and anointed himself, he put on clean robes and climbed on to his throne from where his glory blazed out over the universe, lighting even the abyss itself. The gods all bowed out in front of him. 'Great Lord of the Universe,' they cried. 'Great Lord of the Universe.'

For Marduk had created the universe from the body of Tiamet, the salt water, their mother. Marduk had slain the dragon, made for them a world.

BABYLONIAN

¶ In the beginning one of the gods of heaven stirred the chaotic waters with his staff. When he raised the staff muddy foam dripped down from it, this expanded and thickened, until it formed the islands of Japan. . . .

JAPAN

❡ The universe is round, like a gourd, a calabash, and the earth floats inside it, like a small one within a large. At its beginning the divine serpent carried god here and there in its mouth. The mountains appeared where they stopped at night to rest; they created everything between them. Yet all the waters that god made stood still. So the divine serpent etched out the courses of rivers and the beds of streams; when they began to flow, the earth began to live. Then god said, 'Hold the earth together.' The serpent coiled himself about it, made it firm; it has remained so. Yet the serpent coils, uncoils himself unceasingly. His motion turns our world and sets the planets turning. He moves in quiet pools and running streams, he is the endless undulations of the sea, he is the flash of light across the water.

AFRICA Dahomey

❡ In the beginning human beings lived in the sky and imagined nothing else. But then one day their chief's daughter fell ill. No one knew what was wrong with her, no one could cure her, she lay and suffered day and night. At length the wise old man of the tribe dreamed a strange dream. He came to the people next day and said, 'We must bury the chief's daughter near the great tree that stands by his lodge. Then we must dig it up. The spirit has told me in my dream.' The people murmured for that tree gave them food to eat in the winter when they were hungry. Nonetheless they did exactly as the old man said, carrying the girl there and laying her down, then setting themselves to dig up the great tree. It fell with a crash, its roots in the air, leaving a huge hole where it had been, into which fell the girl who had been lying there asleep – pushed some say by one man who was still angry because of the sacrifice that had been demanded of his people. The girl grabbed at the roots of the tree to save herself. She dragged the tree down with her, through the hole, down, down and down they fell; down and down; and nothing to meet them far below but an endless, endless ocean on which swam water fowl of all kinds, swans and ducks and plovers and divers. These saw her fall and took pity on her plight. Linking themselves

Earth 13

together they made a platform of bone and feather on which she landed, though the tree sank straight to the bottom of the sea. 'She is much too beautiful to drown,' the birds said. 'But she is much too heavy a burden for us to bear for very long. Who will carry this woman now?' 'I will,' said the great turtle chief, and took her on his back at once. Then he said, 'This will bring good fortune to our people. We must make the woman a resting place that will last her for ever and that will be big enough to carry all the other creatures who may join her there. You saw the tree that fell with her, the earth still clinging to its roots. One of you must dive to the bottom of the sea and bring some of that earth to me.'

All the water birds and creatures heard him. But the sea was not only wide but deep. Otter, muskrat and beaver dived in turn, none of them could reach the bottom. As each re-emerged on the surface of the sea he rolled over and died from sheer exhaustion.

At last toad said, 'Now I will try,' but he was gone so long that the others peering down into the depths of the sea and seeing no sign of him thought him wholly lost. At last slowly, slowly, he swam upwards and appeared among the waves around them. He too was so weary he could hardly croak, he rolled over and died at once. But his mouth had fallen open and in it there was a little speck of earth and this the turtle told them to place upon his back. Which they did. Being magic earth it spread and spread until it covered all the turtle's shell, spread and spread onwards till it had made a whole earth, supported still upon the turtle's back, but with room enough on it for any creature who would care to come.

Yet darkness covered it. The animals gathered together again to consider the problem. A lamp was needed, they thought, a great lamp placed high up in the sky, high enough to fill the whole earth with light. But none of them knew how to make such a lamp or how to take it to the sky, or so they said, until the great turtle called the little turtle and she said she might possibly manage to climb the steep and dangerous road into the sky. All the other animals joined their magic to help her. They caused a great black cloud to form and in it were many rocks, which clashing together filled the sky with flashes of lightning. As soon as she saw these the little turtle climbed into the cloud and rode around in it, all over the sky, seizing each lightning flash that passed until she had enough of them to make a golden burning ball, bigger than she was, and this she threw with all her might higher and higher into the sky. And there it stood, the sun. And when the cloud moved on again, she gathered enough lightning to make another ball, a smaller, paler one, which in its turn she threw above her and that one made the moon.

'It is good,' the great turtle said. 'Now the earth has day.' Then he sent the burrowing animals to make holes in the corners of the sky, so that the sun and the moon would be able to circle the earth, descending through one hole and rising up again through the other. When the sky descended the earth grew dark, when it arose it filled with light again. 'Now it has day and night,' said the turtle.

So the earth was created for the sky chief's daughter; she made herself a shelter of branches and lived there safely among the other creatures.

NORTH AMERICA *Iroquois*

¶ In the beginning there was nothing but water, water, water. There was no voice of god, no voice of spirit, no wind, no rocks, no paths, no jungle. As the sky is now, so was water then. On a great lotus leaf that drifted here and there on the waters sat Bhagavan. There was no fruit and flower to his life; he was alone. One day he rubbed his arm and with the dirt that came off he made a crow, his daughter Karicag. When she could fly Bhagavan said to her,

'Go, find some earth for me, I am lonely here; I want to make a world.'

The crow flew and flew and flew and flew, who knows where it went. At last the breath left its body and fell with a thud on the back of Kekramal Chhatri the great tortoise, who was sitting in the water with one arm on the bottom of the ocean and one arm reaching the sky. Kekramal Chhatri said, 'What is the matter? Why are you panting like that?'

'Oh elder brother, I was so tired that life was leaving my body.'

'Where are you going, little sister?'

'I am searching for earth. Where can I find it?'

'Go and look for Gichnaraja, the worm at the bottom of the ocean; it is he who has swallowed the earth. I will take you to Logundi Raja who will help you.'

So Kekramal Chhatri took the crow to Logundi Raja and the Raja called the twelve brothers Loharsur, the thirteen brothers Tamersur and the fourteen brothers Agyasur, and they made a great iron cage with windows. Kekramal Chhatri and the crow got into the cage, and Logundi Raja lowered them till they reached the bottom of the ocean. He gave them another chain in their hands and said, 'When you are ready, pull this and I'll haul you up.'

Gichnaraja was sleeping; the cage landed near his head. Kekramal Chhatri and the crow came out and woke him up. He was very angry.

'I've slept for twelve years,' he shouted, 'and now you've broken my sleep. I've had no food all that time, so now I'm going to eat you.'

Kekramal Chhatri got behind the crow when he heard that.

'Whose daughter are you?' the worm asked them.

'I am the daughter of Bhagavan.'

'Why have you come here?'

'I have come to find the earth.'

'Did your father put the earth here so that you could come and look for it?'

When she heard that the crow was very angry and said, 'If you don't give me the earth, bhosari, I'll beat you.'

That made Gichnaraja frightened, and he said, 'The earth isn't here, my daughter, it's over there, but it's guarded by a Dano who will burn you to ashes if you go near him.' So said Gichnaraja.

But Kekranal Chhatri didn't believe this pretence: when he saw that the worm was afraid, he forgot to be afraid himself and he came out from behind the crow's back and jumped on the worm and seized him by the neck.

'Give me the earth at once, or I'll cut off your head.' So said Kekramal Chhatri. So he began to squeeze and squeeze. The worm wriggled and twisted this way and that, and screamed.

'My son, my son, wait a moment.' He began to vomit then.

Twenty-one times he vomited. Each time he brought up some earth, each time it was about the size of a berry.

His first vomit brought up Dharti Mai, mother earth; his second Piri Dharti, Yellow Earth; his third Kari Dharti, Black Earth; his fourth Papi Dharti, Sinful Earth where a tiger can kill you; his fifth Muhamundi Dharti, arid land where you sow but get no harvest; his sixth, Mudh Maili Dharti, where a woman has her periods; his seventh Chutahi Dharti, Untouched Earth; his eighth Dudhia Dharti, earth white as milk; his ninth Dharni Dharti, the good earth; his tenth Chamkan Dharti, the earth that quakes; his eleventh, Beri Dharti, where all kinds of earth are mixed; his twelfth Alo Dharti, red earth; his thirteenth, Nangi Dharti, naked earth; his fourteenth, Gori Dharti, white earth; his fifteenth Pahari Dharti, rocky earth; his sixteenth, Dharra Dharti, red gravel earth; his seventeenth, Sahri Dharti; his eighteenth, Dhairi, deaf earth; his nineteenth, Anna Kuari, fertile earth that gives grain; his twentieth, Utkan Dharti, earth where nothing grows; his twenty-first Kuari Dharti, virgin soil.

Gichnaraja gave all the earth to the crow, and Kekramal Chhatri tugged at the chain and Logundi Raja pulled the two of them up. Kekramal Chhatri tied the earth round the crow's neck with a rope, and the crow flew away, away, away; she nearly died of weariness; till at last she came home to Bhagavan.

'Have you brought the earth, my daughter?' he asked when he saw her.

'Yes, father, I have.'

Then Bhagavan undid the earth from the crow's neck and put it in his lap. Then he called a young virgin. She made a pot out of leaves, and put the earth in it, and she churned it. For eight days and nine nights she churned till all was ready. Then Bhagavan rolled the earth out like a great chapati and spread it on the face of the waters. Then it began to grow till it covered all the waters.

INDIA *Baiga*

The Song of the World

¶ In the beginning there was only darkness everywhere – darkness and water. And the darkness gathered thick in places, crowding together and then separating, crowding and separating until at last out of one of the places where the darkness had crowded there came forth a man. This man wandered through the darkness until he began to think; then he knew himself and that he was a man; he knew that he was there for some purpose.

He put his hand over his heart and drew forth a large stick. He used the stick to help him through the darkness, and when he was weary he rested upon it. Then he made for himself little ants; he brought them from his body and put them on the stick. Everything that he made he drew from his own body even as he had drawn the stick from his heart. The stick was of grease-wood, and of the gum of the wood the ants made a round ball upon the stick. Then the man took the ball from the stick and put it down in the darkness under his foot, and as he stood upon the ball he rolled it under his foot and sang:

> 'I make the world, and lo!
> The world is finished.
> Thus I make the world, and lo!
> The world is finished.'

So he sang, calling himself the maker of the world. He sang slowly, and all the while the ball grew larger as he rolled it, till at the end of his song, it was the world. Then he sang more quickly:

> 'Let it go, let it go,
> Let it go, start it forth!'

So the world was made, and now the man brought from himself a rock and divided it into little pieces. Of these he made stars, and put them in the sky to light the darkness. But the stars were not bright enough.

So he made Tau-muk, the milky-way. Yet Tau-muk was not bright enough. Then he made the moon. All these he made of rocks drawn forth from himself. But even the moon was not bright enough. So he began to wonder what next he could do. He could bring nothing from himself that could lighten the darkness.

Then he thought. And from himself he made two large bowls, and he filled the one with water and covered it with the other. He sat and watched the bowls, and while he watched he wished that what he wanted to make in very truth would come to be. And it was even as he wished. For the water in the bowl turned into the sun and shone out in rays through the cracks where the bowls joined.

When the sun was made, the man lifted off the top bowl and took out the sun and threw it to the east. But the sun did not touch the ground; it stayed in the sky where he threw it and never moved. Then in the same way he threw the sun to the north and to the west and to the south. But each time it only stayed in the sky, motionless, for it never touched the ground. Then he threw it once more to the east, and this time it touched the ground and bounced and started upward. Since then the sun has never ceased to move. It goes around the world in a day, but every morning it must bounce anew in the east.

NORTH AMERICA *Chuhwuht*

¶ At first there was no earth and sky; there were only two great eggs. But they were not ordinary eggs, for they were soft and shone like gold. At last, as they went round they collided, and both the eggs broke open. From one came the Earth, from the other the Sky, her husband.

Now the Earth was too big for the Sky to hold in his arms and he said, 'Though you are my wife, you are greater than I and I cannot take you. Make yourself smaller.'

The Earth accordingly made herself pliable and the mountains and valleys were formed, and she became small and the Sky was able to go to her in love.

When the Sky made love to the Earth, every kind of tree and grass and all living creatures came into being.

INDIA *Hrusso*

¶ There was a virgin once, very beautiful, daughter of the Air. She lived all alone in the Air's wide and windy mansions, wandering alone from one hall to another. She was a young girl in feeling but no one kept her company, and the time went on it seemed to her for ever and for ever.

So she left Air's empty palaces and sank down till she met the empty waves of the sea. At first they rocked her gently. Then a storm arose, its furious winds drove her this way and that across their angry billowing. Yet when wind and water calmed they made as if they loved her. They loved her so much she grew big with their child.

Yet she never gave birth. For seven whole centuries she bore the pain and weight of this child of wind and water. She swam east and west, to northwest and southeast, the child thundering inside her – oh why, she wept at last, this mother of the water, oh why must I endure it? Why must I wander, tossed by salt water, driven by the wind? Far better to return to my father's empty mansions. Oh Ukko, great god, come and free me from my torment.

A little while after a teal came flying, quietly and slowly, searching for somewhere to make herself a nest. She flew to west and east, to northeast and southwest, saw nothing but sea, nowhere to settle. The Mother of Water took pity on her wanderings, she rose from the waves, and crooked her knees to make a lap; the teal saw it thankfully as a peaceful green island. She laid six golden eggs in the nest she made, a seventh of iron. All the three days she brooded them the mother's lap grew warmer – on the fourth her knees began to burn, their sinews seemed to melt, their veins filled with fire, she could not stop them trembling violently. The eggs rolled off them one by one, fell down into the sea and shattered to fragments.

Yet no part of them was wasted, golden or iron – not yolk nor white nor shell – all were beautiful in making. Half one eggshell formed the earth itself, its upper half arched the heavens over it. Its yolk made the golden sun, its white became the moon, its specklings were stars, its darker parts the clouds.

And still the Mother of Water lay rocking on the ocean. She had the sun by day to warm her and the moon's white beams came to comfort her at night. She rested for nine years; in the tenth she raised her head, began the business of creation. She put out one hand and there were all the headlands. She dipped her feet in the ocean and so made caves for fishes. She dived deep beneath the sea, with both hands formed its bed. She turned her head towards the land and extended the level shores, she made beaches and bays along it and good places for fishing. She planted rocks and reefs at sea to await unwary sailors.

So all the islands were made and the rocks and reefs about them and the four mighty pillars that held the sky from falling. She made islands and continents, engraved rocks and split the hills, she twisted the mountains and lifted up their summits.

And still the child remained unborn to her. He had grown old there in her womb, his dwelling as narrow as his mother's once was wide in her father's empty mansions. He felt no warmth from the sun, saw no light from sun or moon. Nor did they answer when he called on them to help him. 'Let me out ... let me out ...' he called and called; they would not answer anything.

For seven whole centuries Vainamoienen lived within his mother. Now he reached his hands to meet the bone of her passageway, he pushed out both his feet, parted his knees widely. Thrusting her body open he forged himself an exit, forced out into the air, fell headlong to the sea.

It was Vainamoienen who saw first the world his mother had created, with its rocks and headlands, islands and mountains. It was he who clothed it. He, Vainamoienen, sowed the seeds that bore trees and grasses, the cherries and junipers, all the fruits and flowers.

FINLAND

From the conception the increase
From the increase the swelling
From the swelling the thought
From the thought the remembrance
From the remembrance the consciousness, the desire.
The word became fruitful:

It dwelt with the feeble glimmering
It brought forth night;
The great night, the long night,
The lowest night, the loftiest night
The thick night, the night to be felt
The night touched, the night unseen,
The night following,
The night ending in death
From the nothing, the begetting,
From the nothing, the increase
From the nothing, the abundance,
The power of increasing, the living breath;
It dwelt with the empty space
It produced the atmosphere which is above us,
The atmosphere which floats above the earth
The great firmament above us
The spread out space dwelt into the early dawn,
Then the moon sprang forth;
The atmosphere above dwelt into the glowing sky,
Forthwith was produced the sun,
They were thrown up above as the chief eyes of Heaven:
Then the Heavens became light, the early dawn, the
    early day,
The sky floats above the earth
Dwelt into Hawaiki
And produced islands, Taporapora, Tauwari, Nikan
    and Kukapapa
Wawauetea and Wiwhi te rangi and Ragi.

NEW ZEALAND Maori

¶ . . . Seti-Melo set himself to put the world in order. In one place
he made it flat, in another he piled up the hills. He made the rivers
flow between them. When he had finished he came to Assam and
while he was resting there he caused the English to be created. . . .

INDIA Rori

MAN

What a piece of work is a man . . .

Shakespeare

. . . But who is stronger than death?
me, evidently.
Pass, Crow.

Ted Hughe

Thus; earth was created first, then man to live on it. Or could it be the other way about – was earth created rather to house man? A second, related questions asks: is the form in which we find ourselves a perfected one? Or is it just a pale reflection of what we once were in some golden age – and could be again, perhaps, if we worked at it?

The more familiar of the two Biblical accounts sees man as created last in order to people the already prepared earth. Whereas in the second, sometimes overlooked, the one included here, God makes man first and then decorates the earth on his behalf. Just so, other mythologies – many American Indian stories in particular – show man arriving to find at best a barren surface, at worst nothing at all, earth having to be dredged up for him from the bottom of the sea. Frequently too in these stories his own progression is upwards, an ascent. Indeed the Mayan Indian story (like another one here from Borneo) makes this progression actually substantial; first wood then clay are tried and found wanting as material for man's making; finally the gods mould him, bone and flesh and blood, from the maize flour; which is an interesting inversion of the story of the slain man from whose body the maize first grows. (See Part Six, The Origin of Food Plants.)

In the Mayan story, typically enough, the gods are shown as literally makers, creating man as a weaver weaves cloth or a potter moulds pots out of clay: especially as a potter moulds pots out of clay. For if the Mayan gods rejected clay as a material, elsewhere earth or clay or sand, the mother substance, is the one most frequently chosen by man's creator. (So it is in the second Genesis account – indeed the name Adam in its root form means not only man but also red earth.) Sometimes, however, no material may be specified at all, the creator god may not even make man with his own hands. His function may simply be to donate his life force; either his breath, his seed, or else, significantly, that other life force, his blood. This last is perhaps the most fundamental idea of all, possibly the most widespread – even if the blood used is not always the god's own. (In the extract from The Koran, *for instance, its origin is unstated, as it is with the blood-streaked flower in the Mandan Indian story, though that clearly is also meant as an image of the birth process.) Indirectly it is the theme of the Mayan story too. For if maize had sprung from blood in the first place it could of course make the blood of the true and perfect man – an example of mythical logic at its most simple and beautiful.*

Man   25

When God came to the earth to prepare the present order of things, he found three beings there, the thunder, an elephant, and a Dorobo, all living together.

One day the thunder remarked: 'What sort of a creature is this man? If he wishes to turn over from one side to the other when he is asleep, he is able to do so. If I wish to turn over, I have first of all to get up.'

The elephant said: 'It is the same with me; before I can turn over from one side to the other, I have to stand up.'

The thunder declared that he was afraid of the man and said he would run away and go to the heavens. At this the elephant laughed and inquired why he was running away, for the man after all was only a small creature. 'But he is bad,' the thunder replied, 'he can turn over when asleep'; and with that he fled and went to the heavens, where he has remained ever since.

The man seeing the thunder go away was pleased, and said: 'The person I was afraid of has fled. I do not mind the elephant.' He then went to the woods and made some poison into which he dipped an arrow, and having cut a bow, he returned to the kraal, and shot the elephant.

The elephant wept and lifted his trunk to the heavens, crying out to the thunder to take him up.

The thunder refused, however, and said: 'I shall not take you, for when I warned you that the man was bad, you laughed and said he was small.'

The elephant cried out again and begged to be taken to heaven, as he was on the point of death.

But the thunder only replied: 'Die by yourself.'

And the elephant died, and the man became great in all the countries.

AFRICA, KENYA Nandi

In the day that the Lord God made the earth, and the heavens, and every plant of the field, before it was in the earth, and every herb of the field, before it grew: for the Lord God had not caused it to rain upon the earth, and there was not a man to till the ground. But there went up a mist from the earth, and watered the whole face of the ground. And the Lord God formed man of the dust of the ground, and breathed into his nostrils the breath of life; and man became a living soul.

And the Lord God planted a garden Eastward in Eden; and there he put the man whom he had formed. And out of the ground made the Lord God to grow every tree that is pleasant to the sight, and good for food: the tree of life also in the midst of the garden, and the tree of knowledge of good and evil. And a river went out of Eden to water the garden, and from thence it was parted, and became into four heads. The name of the first is Pison: that is it which compasseth the whole land of Havilah. And the name of the second river is Gihon: the same is it that compasseth the whole land of Ethiopia. And the name of the third river is Hiddekel: that is it which goeth toward the East of Assyria: and the fourth river is Euphrates.

And the Lord God took the man, and put him into the garden of Eden, to dress it, and to keep it. And the Lord God commanded the man, saying, 'Of every tree of the garden thou mayest freely eat. But of the tree of the knowledge of good and evil, thou shalt not eat of it: for in the day that thou eatest thereof, thou shalt surely die.'

And the Lord God said, 'It is not good that the man should be alone: I will make him an helpmeet for him.' And out of the ground the Lord God formed every beast of the field, and every fowl of the air, and brought them unto Adam, to see what he would call them: and whatsoever Adam called every living creature, that was the name thereof. And Adam gave names to all cattle, and to the fowl of the air, and to every beast of the field: but for Adam there was not found an helpmeet for him.

And the Lord God caused a deep sleep to fall upon Adam, and he slept; and he took one of his ribs, and closed up the flesh instead thereof. And the rib which the Lord God had taken from man, made he a woman, and brought her unto the man.

And Adam said, 'This is now bone of my bones, and flesh of my flesh: she shall be called woman, because she was taken out of man.'

Therefore shall a man leave his father and his mother, and shall cleave unto his wife: and they shall be one flesh. And they were both naked, the man and his wife, and were not ashamed.

The Old Testament *The Book of Genesis*, 2: 4-11, 13-25

¶ So God created Adam. His body was made of earth; his bones of stone; his ligaments of roots, his blood of water, his eyes of the sun, his thoughts of cloud, his spirit of wind, his warmth of fire.

RUSSIA

¶ In the beginning there was only Mavutsinim. No one lived with him. He had no wife. He had no son nor did he have any relatives. He was all alone. One day he turned a shell into a woman, and he married her. When his son was born, he asked his wife, 'Is it a man or a woman?'

'It is a man.'

'I'll take him with me.'

Then he left. The boy's mother cried and went back to her village, the lagoon, where she turned into a shell again.

'We are the grandchildren of Mavutsinim's son,' say the Indians.

SOUTH AMERICA, BRAZIL *Xingu*

¶ The moon created the first man and woman. He made man from stone, decorated his body with white and black ashes. But woman he made from the box tree, he rendered her soft and supple by rubbing her with yams and mud.

AUSTRALIA, QUEENSLAND

¶ When they divided the Man, into how many parts did they disperse him? What became of his mouth, what of his arms, what were his two thighs and his two feet called? His mouth was the brahmin, his arms were made into nobles, his two thighs were the populace and from his feet the servants were born.

INDIA *Hindi*

¶ When the God Ulgen created earth he set seven trees on it and under them seven men, a man for each tree. On the golden mountain he put an eighth tree and an eighth man, whom he named Maidere, and then he went away. Seven years passed. Each tree grew seven branches, one branch for each year, but each man remained just as he was, showed no increase.

'How is that?' asked God. 'How can they increase,' said Maidere, 'when they have no woman?' 'Then you'd better come down from your golden mountain and make them one,' said God. So Maidere came down from his golden mountain, and started to create woman. But he could only fashion her body, he could not breathe life into it. Off he went to find Ulgen, leaving Dog on guard. 'Don't let anyone near her,' he said. 'If anyone appears, show your teeth, bark as loud as you can and frighten them away.'

'Right, right,' said Dog.

But hardly was Maidere out of sight when along came Erlik, the devil. 'How would you like a fur coat,' he said to Dog. For Dog was naked in those days and the wind was pretty cold in winter.

'Suppose it wears out? And won't it be too hot for me in summer?' asked Dog.

'No indeed. It'll last you to your dying day. And in summer you'll be cool as a cucumber.'

'So, what do you want me to do?' said Dog.

'I only want to look at what your master has made. That's all I want.'

'Right. Right,' said Dog.

Erlik crept up to the woman. He took out a seven-toned flute and blew into her nose with it. He took out a nine-stringed instrument

Man 29

and blew into her ear with that. She sat up at once and was alive; she had spirit and she had mind, but she had seven tempers beside and nine moods as Dog discovered immediately because she threw a stone at him.

Maidere returned home at this point carrying breath from God, too late, the woman didn't need it now.

'Didn't I tell you not to let anyone near her?' he said to Dog.

'I was cold. Erlik promised me a fur coat, that's more than you ever did,' said Dog.

'Well and good,' said Maidere. 'Let the fur coat grow on your back. And so it will for ever. But I curse you too. They'll always throw stones at you now and treat you badly.'

'Right. Right,' said Dog. And so it was.

RUSSIA *Altai Tartar*

¶ The gods spoke. By their word they made heaven and earth and clothed the earth with trees and grass, with all kinds of bushes and plants. They made animals to live on the earth. But the animals did not know how to praise their maker, they could only howl and hiss and roar and croak and cackle, they could not speak the name of God. The gods said, 'Because they are not able to praise us, they shall rend each other with tooth and claw and feed off each other's flesh for ever.'

Next the gods took clay and fashioned man from that. But these men could not move or speak, they were too soft to stand upright or to turn their heads. When the rains fell their substance melted and was clay again. So the gods made men from wood instead, and they moved and danced and spoke and reproduced themselves. But they had no minds, no souls, and not knowing who had created them, did not worship their creators; sometimes even they fell on all fours and walked like beasts. 'It is not good,' said the gods, and caused a flood to sweep them off the face of the earth. Afterwards they took counsel for a long time. And then, sending for the jaguar and the coyote, the parrot and the crow, they ordered them to gather together the special food, the white and yellow maize; they pounded it, and from the flour made men; thus food was man's body, his blood was the maize and as it was true and special food, this was at last true man. There were four men at first, as there are four corners of the world, and four women the gods had created for the men. They had minds and hearts, their eyes could see far off, they knew the gods who made them, and they honoured them properly.

CENTRAL AMERICA *Maya*

¶ There was once a spirit named Towadakon. He said, 'I will make a human being.' So he took the trunk of a Tambohilik tree and smoothed it, and made a man from it. When he had made a man he told him to call aloud but he couldn't. Then Towadakon said, 'I do not want this because it cannot do anything.' Afterwards he made a man from stone. He told it to call aloud and it could do so; he told it to speak and it couldn't; he told it to dance and it didn't know how to. So he threw it away and, as the wooden man and the stone man had not succeeded, he made one of earth. When it was finished he told it to call aloud and it could; he told it to talk and it could talk, when he told it to dance it did so, when he told it to laugh, it could laugh, and thus it became the first man.

NORTH BORNEO *Dusuns*

¶ Tane wanted a wife and children. But he knew of only one woman, his mother Papa, and she said to him, 'You can't marry me, no good will come of it. See if your ancestress Mumuhango will have you.' So Tane married Mumuhango and soon she was pregnant. Tane was delighted. But when her time came Mumuhango did not give birth to a man, only a totara-tree. Tane wept and went back to his mother. Papa said, 'Well I can see that it is not altogether satisfactory, how about your ancestress Hine-tu-a-maunga instead? She lives on the mountain.' So Tane climbed the mountain and married his ancestress Hine-tu-a-maunga, and she became pregnant in her turn, but she too produced no man-child only rusty water and a mountain lizard. Tane went back to his mother, Papa. 'I am sorry for you my son,' she said. 'Try your ancestress Rangahore.' But Rangahore's child was a round stone. 'Then try your ancestress Ngaore. She is tender and gentle.' But Ngaore gave birth to tender and gentle rushes. So it was with all Tane's wives, not one of them gave him a man-child. Tane wept, he said to his mother, 'I will never have a child in my own image.' 'You give up too easily. Can't you hear your ancestor Ocean muttering away in the distance, why don't you go and pay him a visit?' 'I can't marry my ancestor, Ocean,' said Tane. 'No indeed you can't. But you can marry the woman you make yourself beside him. Scrape up the sand and see what you will see.'

So Tane followed the muttering of the ocean and soon he came down to the beach at Hawaiki, and squatted there right at the edge of the sea. He put out a hand. He put out both his hands. He gathered up sand and mixed it with mud to make it firm. He smoothed it and rounded it. He made a head, he made legs, he made arms and a belly. Soon the figure of a woman lay complete before him. Tane touched her all over, because he had made her, then he laid her down and covering her with a garment, bent and kissed her, breathing gently into her very mouth. Afterwards he left her, without another glance, without a word. He went to his mother and said, 'She is finished.' 'Go back,' Papa said, 'and see what you will see.' So Tane returned to the beach. The woman sat up. She stood up. She stood with the waves about her feet, trembling and gazing this way and that. As soon as she saw Tane she began to laugh, and he went to her, smiling, and put out his hand to her. She became his wife. She gave birth to his children, and the third among them was a man, a human child.

NEW ZEALAND *Maori*

¶ Demons flew over the darkness, and amidst fearful noise the Great and Strong said, 'Be still!'

The demons were dumb, sound died away and there was complete silence.

'First, let there be Earth,' said the powerful Alla, 'and then I will create Heaven and Light.'

The Almighty blew, and the vapour of his breath became stones which grew into mountains; when the mountains had reached an immense height, they were overthrown and plains were formed.

Looking at the Earth which he had created, Alla rejoiced.

'It is well,' he said; 'there shall be people on it.'

But he remembered Heaven; he must create Heaven.

Alla's eyes flashed, and the air from his eyes flamed and burned; darkness changed to light.

The Lord ordered the fire to melt stones.

As the stones burned, green smoke from them stretched upwards and the firmament of Heaven was formed in seven rows.

Alla was pleased with the created Heaven.

'Heaven is yet finer than Earth,' he said; 'it is well for people to live on Earth, but life for my prophets shall be even better.'

Having made small balls out of the firmament, Alla blew upon each of them; the balls whirled and (how wonderful are the deeds of Alla!) grew into human form.

After a time they ceased, like the dead, to grow any more.

Then the Almighty introduced sacred fire into each of the statues and said:

'My prophets, hear me!'

Hearing the cry of Alla, the prophets fell face downwards and wept and said:

'We hear, we hear!'

The Lord descended on to the Earth.

Taking a handful of soil into each hand, he blew on it and said:

'Earth, I am your Lord.'

From his open right hand there fell upon the Earth a ball which twisted round and gradually assumed human form.

Alla did not introduce the sacred fire into man after the manner in which he had introduced it into the prophets, but touched man and said, 'Live!'

Then opening his closed left hand, he in a similar way created woman.

Alla called man Yadym and woman Ava.

'I have given you the whole Earth,' he said to the first people, 'but alone you will not succeed on it. The presence of many people is necessary in order to employ the Earth to advantage and to preserve it.'

'You, Ava,' thus Alla commanded the woman, 'must bear people and beget as many as possible.'

And strong Alla directed the man to unite with the woman and to beget children.

'Omnipotent Spirit!' said the first man, 'how shall we live?'

The Great smiled, and seizing a stone, squeezed it so powerfully with his hands that water flowed. Much water ran from the stone and formed enormous rivers and lakes, into which Alla threw a handful of earth; such earth became fish.

'Catch and eat them when you are hungry,' said the Almighty.

He took green smoke from Heaven and coloured Earth with it; the Earth became covered with grass and trees. The trees grew and flowers and fruit appeared on the trees.

'The fruits are for your use and comfort,' said the Lord to the people.

And the first people rejoiced and said, 'How good it is for us to live with You! We are happy!'

'Wait, I have not created all,' said Alla graciously. 'I will give you assistants and labourers.'

He took clay into his hands and created animals and birds.

A bear growled ferociously and frightened people so that they ran away, but Alla stopped them and told them to approach the bear without fear. Yadym advanced and the bear came to his feet as peacefully as a lamb. Ava meanwhile was surrounded by a flock of fat goats and sheep, and fed them from her hands.

The Powerful drew near to her and said:

'Henceforth thus let it be; as the male, you, Yadym, will be brave and strong and the ruler; and you, Ava, must manage the household affairs. Live and use my gifts and be fruitful. I will go to Heaven and observe from there how you live. I will make plenty of windows in Heaven and look through them at the world; you will call these windows stars.'

And great Alla departed to Heaven and stayed there; and Yadym and Ava stayed alone on Earth.

And people began to live.

RUSSIA *Bashkir*

❡ There was nothing but sea. There was nothing but sky; the one arched over the other and a rock fell down from the sky on to the water. Slime covered the rock after a while, and in a little while longer still worms bred from the slime, and bored deep into the rock; the result of their boring was sand which gradually spread over the whole rock and was earth, deep enough for plants, only there were none; until years and years later, a spade handle fell down from the sun and rooted itself in the earth. It grew and grew and when it was a tall and shady tree a vine descended from the moon and embraced it closely and lovingly and from that mating were born a boy and a girl; who in their turn grew up, were wedded and became the parents of people upon earth.

NORTH BORNEO *Kyan*

❡ Sing-Bonga made a boy and girl. Between them, he thought, they would people the world. He put them in a cave and waited for the children to come. But they did not. The boy and girl knew nothing, nothing came of it. Sing-Bonga went away and thought again. He thought and thought – in a little while he had invented rice beer and taught them how to make it, they had twelve sons and twelve daughters in no time at all.

INDIA *Kol*

❡ We first created man from an essence of clay: then placed him, a living germ, in a safe enclosure. The germ we made a clot of blood, and the clot a lump of flesh. This we fashioned into bones, then

Man 35

clothed the bones with flesh, thus bringing forth another creation. Blessed be Allah, the noblest of creators.

MOSLEM The Koran

¶ There were no men once, only a Being. And one day this Being scratched out on the ground the figures of two men. But they did not move at all. So he took a knife and cut himself and sprinkled the two figures with his blood, then he covered them over with coconut leaves and went away and left them. In a little while the leaves stirred. They were pushed aside. Up sprang the two heroes, To-Kabinana and To-Karvuvu. But they were alone now and lonely, they wanted company. So To-Kabinana climbed a coconut tree right to the very top where the coconuts are, and he threw down two fine yellow coconuts, and when these hit the ground they burst open and turned into two beautiful women to be his wives and keep him company. To-Karvuvu saw them, he wanted wives too, but did not know how to get them. 'Then how did you find your wives?' he asked To-Kabinana. 'You must climb a coconut tree,' said his brother, 'pick two yellow nuts and throw them down carefully.' So To-Karvuvu in his turn climbed a coconut palm, up, up to the top where the coconuts grew and he too picked two coconuts and threw them to the gound. But he was in such a hurry he picked darker coconuts, in such a hurry he threw them down carelessly, so that they fell on their undersides. And again the coconuts split open and again they turned into women. But they were not beautiful women like To-Kabinana's wives, they had flat noses and dark skins, they were really very ugly indeed. To-Karvuvu would have nothing to do with them. He took one of his brother's beautiful fair-skinned wives instead. And the women To-Karvuvu had made gave birth to the dark-skinned people. It was all To-Karvuvu's fault, To-Kabinana said, for choosing his coconuts so carelessly.

MELANESIA New Hebrides

⁊ All the world was empty and among the waters walked Lone Man. He knew nothing. He did not know where he came from, how he had been born. He went back, following his own track across the water, and at last found a flower striped red with blood. 'I gave birth to you,' she said. 'You were born to wander the world for all your life.' But there was only water, there was no world. Lone Man knew there must be something more; to have given his mother life; and if not how could he find a place to live? When he met two ducks he ordered them to dive and fetch earth from the bottom of the sea. This they did. They brought up four pieces and placed them between his hands. He threw them out upon the waters and they lay there in the four directions and gave grass and fruit and trees to him.

NORTH AMERICA *Mandan*

⁊ Ea said: 'I will join blood to blood and that blood to bone. I will create my own being to adore me. His name is Man.' But he said, 'I will need one life for my creation.' The other gods chose Kingu, the rebel leader, Tiamet's captain. They held him down and bound him and cut open all his veins. With the blood that flowed out of Kingu's veins Ea created man, to be his servant and to worship him.

BABYLONIAN

⁊ At the beginning of Things, when there was nothing, neither man, nor animals, nor plants, nor heaven, nor earth, nothing, nothing, God *was* and he was called Nzame. The three who are Nzame, we call them Nzame, Mebere, and Nkwa. At the beginning Nzame made the heaven and the earth and he reserved the heaven for himself. Then he blew on to the earth, and earth and water were created, each on its side.

Nzame made everything: heaven, earth, sun, moon, stars, animals, plants; everything. When he had finished everything that we see today, he called Mebere and Nkwa and showed them his work.

'This is my work. Is it good?'

They replied, 'Yes, you have done well.'

'Does anything remain to be done?'

Mebere and Nkwa answered him, 'We see many animals, but we do not see their chief; we see many plants, but we do not see their master.'

As masters for all these things, they appointed the elephant, because he had wisdom; the leopard, because he had power and cunning; and the monkey, because he had malice and suppleness.

But Nzame wanted to do even better; and between them he, Mebere, and Nkwa created a being almost like themselves. One gave him force, the second sway, and the third beauty. Then the three of them said:

'Take the earth. You are henceforth the master of all that exists. Like us you have life, all things belong to you, you are the master.'

Nzame, Mebere, and Nkwa returned to the heights to their dwelling place, and the new creature remained below alone, and everything obeyed him. But among all the animals, the elephant remained the first, the leopard the second, and the monkey the third, because it was they whom Mebere and Nkwa had first chosen.

Nzame, Mebere, and Nkwa called the first man Fam – which means power.

Proud of his sway, his power, and his beauty, because he surpassed in these three qualities the elephant, the leopard, and the monkey, proud of being able to defeat all the animals, this first man grew wicked; he became arrogant, and did not want to worship Nzame again; and he scorned him:

> Yeye, o, layeye,
> God on high, man on the earth,
> Yeye, o, layeye,
> God is God,
> Man is man,
> Everyone in his house, everyone for himself!

God heard the song. 'Who sings?' he asked.

'Look for him,' cried Fam.

'Who sings?'

'Yeye, o, layeye!'

'Who sings?'

'Eh! it is me!' cried Fam.

Furious, God called Nzalan, the thunder. 'Nzalan, come!' Nzalan came running with great noise: *boom, boom, boom!* The fire of heaven fell on the forest. The plantations burnt like vast torches. *Foo, foo, foo!* – everything in flames. The earth was then, as today, covered with forests. The trees burnt; the plants, the bananas, the cassava, even the pistachio nuts, everything dried up; animals, birds, fishes, all were destroyed, everything was dead. But when God had created the first man, he had told him, 'You will never die.' And what God gives he does not take away. The first man was burnt, but none knows what became of him. He is alive, yes, but where?

But God looked at the earth, all black, without anything, and idle; he felt ashamed and wanted to do better. Nzeme, Mebere, and Nkwa took counsel and they did as follows: over the black earth covered with coal they put a new layer of earth; a tree grew, grew bigger and bigger and when one of its seeds fell down a new tree was born, when a leaf severed itself it grew and grew and began to walk. It was an animal, an elephant, a leopard, an antelope, a tortoise – all of them. When a leaf fell into the water it swam, it was a fish, a sardine, a crab, an oyster – all of them. The earth became again what it had been, and what it still is today. The proof that this is the truth is this: when one digs up the earth in certain places, one finds a hard black stone which breaks; throw it in the fire and it burns.

But Nzame, Mebere, and Nkwa took counsel again; they needed a chief to command all the animals. 'We shall make a man like Fam,' said Nzame, 'the same legs and arms, but he shall turn his head and he shall see death.'

This was the second man and the father of all. Nzame called him *Sekume*, but did not want to leave him alone, and said, 'Make yourself a woman from a tree.'

Sekume made himself a woman and she walked and he called her *Mbongwe*.

When Nzame made Sekume and Mbongwe he made them in two parts, an outer part called Gnoul, the body, and the other which lives in the body, called Nsissim.

Nsissim is that which produces the shadow, Nsissim is the shadow – it is the same thing. It is Nsissim who makes Gnoul live. Nsissim goes away when man dies, but Nsissim does not die. Do you know where he lives? He lives in the eye. The little shining point you see in the middle, that is Nsissim.

> Stars above
> Fire below
> Coal in the hearth
> The soul in the eye
> Cloud smoke and death.

Sekume and Mbongwe lived happily on earth and had many children. But Fam, the first man, was imprisoned by God under the earth. With a large stone he blocked the entrance. But the malicious Fam tunnelled at the earth for a long time, and one day, at last, he was outside! Who had taken his place? The new man. Fam was furious with him. Now he hides in the forest to kill them, under the water to capsize their boats.

> Remain silent,
> Fam is listening,
> To bring misfortune;
> Remain silent.

AFRICA, GABON *Fang*

¶ In the beginning there were three hills and two beings of different sexes but without earthly appetites born of these parents, the water and the earth. The Creator named them Yatam and Yatai and watched them for a while. He decided that they would make good parents for mankind. So he dropped three gourds from heaven and the two beings became hungry and ate them, all but the seeds which they spat out and planted by a big rock. After three months and seven days the seeds had grown into two large creepers. After three years and seven months they had blossomed and each creeper produced a gourd which swelled and swelled until it was the size of a large hill, only not silent as a hill is silent, for from the one came the sound of all the animals, whistles and hisses, croaks and grunts and growls, from the other could be heard the voices of mankind, shouting and whispering, laughing and crying.

Yatam and Yatai meanwhile had discovered the pleasure of sexual union. Thus as the two gourds swelled so did Yatai; until at last she gave birth to a girl with tiger's legs and tiger's ears. Her parents named her Wang Pyekkha Yek-khi and gave into her care their parents, the water and the earth, and the two gourds, each the size of a hill, one containing all the animals, the other all mankind. Whoever shall split these gourds, they said to her, shall be your husband and rule the world with you.

At this time a man was wandering the earth. He had come down from heaven once but eaten so much rice he had grown too heavy to return there. His name was Hkun Hsang L'rong. In due course of time he came to the place where Yatam and Yatai and their daughter lived, and he promptly fell in love with Wang Pyekkha Yek-khi, charmed by her tiger legs and her tiger ears, and asked if he might marry her. Only if you can split these two gourds, her parents told him.

Hkun Hsang L'rong prayed aloud to the two great beings in heaven. 'I have wandered a long time,' he cried. 'I have made a great pilgrimage. If I am who I think I am, if I am destined to become the very Buddha himself, send me from heaven the celestial sword, the great two-handed one.'

The two beings in heaven heard his prayer. They sent him the magic two-edged sword. He lifted it, shouted a warning to all the animals inside, struck the first gourd and split it open; only the crab did not get out of the way in time, so was split in half bloodlessly and has remained in half, bloodless, to this very day. All the other animals emerged safely, whistling or hissing, croaking or grunting or growling. Then Hkun Hsang L'rong raised the two-edged sword again, shouted and struck and split the second gourd in two. And out came all the sixty races of mankind, the kinds that live on rice and the kinds on maize, the kinds on roots and the kinds on flesh, men who shouted and whispered, laughed and cried. In the beginning that was how all animals, that was how men were made.

INDO-CHINA *Wa*

¶ Ohrmazd was god the creator; Ahriman, the devil, his opponent. Ohrmazd created Gosh, the primal bull, and Gayomart, the primal man; the aim of Ahriman on the other hand was to destroy them both. This Ohrmazd knew. The bull and the man stood by the River Daiti, Gayomart helped and fed by Gosh, together they withstood the evil Ahriman was attempting to spread throughout the world. So he turned his war against them and soon both were killed, though Ohrmazd eased the pain of their dying. Gayomart with his final breath said, 'Good will triumph nonetheless. Mankind will be born of me, you shall see.'

Where the bull's blood spilled on to the earth grew trees and grasses, all the flowers and fruit. His seed flew as high as the moon and so all the animals were born. Gayomart's blood lay quieter: for forty years it fertilised the soil, until at last a tall reed grew which opened revealed a woman and a man so closely joined it was not possible to divide them. And when after a time they were put apart they stayed apart for fifty years and then they joined again and from their union a boy and a girl were born. But their parents loved them too much to be separated from them, they wanted their children once more within their own bodies. The man took the boy and the woman the girl and they devoured them.

God said: they love too greatly. And he put his hand on them and reduced the love they bore by ninety-nine per cent. Afterwards they had seven more pairs of children and all these grew to their proper age.

Their parents meanwhile had wandered the world and seen that it was good. 'Ohrmazd created all of it,' they said, 'the waters and the earth, the sun, the moon, the stars, all the fruit and flowers upon the earth.' But Ahriman came and whispered in their minds and afterwards they said, 'Ahriman created all of it, the waters and the earth, the sun and moon and stars, all the fruit and flowers upon the earth.'

That was the first lie: but since the spirit of evil was to blame for it Ohrmazd protected the man and the woman still; showing them how to make fire, how to live comfortably, how to rear their seven pairs of twins. From one of these pairs are descended all the fifteen races of mankind.

PERSIAN

FLOOD

... Who bid'st the mighty ocean deep
   Its own appointed limits keep ...
                        W. Whiting

... And dreaming drowns all men,
collecting them in its cellar,
and the world is washed once more.
                        Pablo Neruda

When Noah is the captain, what is there to fear?
                        Saadi of Shiraz

So, God creates earth and sets man on it. Then not so long after sees fit to wipe him off again – if not by deluge, sometimes by fire instead. Once upon a time, given the Babylonian and Biblical flood myths and also perhaps the Greek one, it could be debated whether they were based on folk memory of an actual historical flood, but too many similar stories have surfaced from every corner of the world to make such theories valid any more. Myself, tentatively, I would ascribe these myths rather to that basic and clearly universal human longing – manifested less dramatically when a man changes jobs or his house – to get rid of an unsatisfying past and start all over again. Hence those expressions – turning over a new leaf, or, more significantly still, wiping the slate clean. Just so a world, post-flood, could be restored to innocence, to another Eden, all bitter experience laid aside, and the history of mankind begin anew.

Of course the causes of flood vary from story to story and culture to culture, not necessarily due to the wickedness of man as it was with Noah's flood. Sometimes the gods could be much more arbitrary. The Babylonians wanted to destroy man just because he was too noisy. Elsewhere one god sends flood in order to curb two quarrelling mountains and it is just man's bad luck he happens to be in the way. Elsewhere still it is caused by some quite inadvertent infringement of some basic law, as when Kitimil, in the Melanesian story, quite reasonably kills the mouse that is eating his sugar-cane. Unfortunately the mouse turns out to be his father-in-law – though Kitimil had been warned of this, one can hardly blame him for not believing it. (Unlike the usual transgressors, however, Kitimil is one of the three people not drowned by the ensuing deluge, which seems both just and unjust at the same time.)

The Chinese story is interesting and typical, at least of other Chinese stories. No need for magic vessels here, whether arks, treetrunks, pumpkins or the carcase of a pigeon as in the oddest of the deluge myths. This flood falls far short of the usual universal holocaust and what it needs to tame it is a good administrator. Hence the divine Yu; who though undoubtedly a magical figure, nevertheless mainly applies the methods of the Civil Service to seeing that the rivers behave themselves in future, and succeeds because – and this takes the myth nearer all the others – he respects the proper heavenly order of things.

For his predecessors had failed to respect that order, thus transgressing
as Kitimil did and maybe, too, those noisy Babylonians.

One last point: not so much in evidence in these stories here, yet
very common and worth noting, is the way Ham, Shem and Japhet in
the Biblical myth are the founders of the different races of mankind.
Just so, many of the other flood myths see the deluge as a fundamental
divide after which once unified mankind splits into many races. Often,
indeed, they all begin speaking different languages after the flood, as
in the Bhil myth here, whereas up till then every man could understand
all the others.

¶ A long time ago the ocean suddenly began to rise, until it covered
the whole land. The water even rose to the top of the mountains
and the ice drifted over them. When the flood had subsided the ice
was stranded and ever since forms an ice cap on top of the mountains. Many shellfish, fish, seals and whales were left high and dry
and their shells and bones may be seen to this day. A great number
of Inuit died during this period, but many others who had taken
to their kayaks when the water commenced to rise were saved.

NORTH AMERICA *Inuit*

¶ You know the city Shurrupak, it stands on the banks of
Euphrates? That city grew old and the gods that were in it were old.
There was Anu, Lord of the firmament, their father, and warrior
Enlil their counsellor, Ninurta the helper, and Ennugi watcher over
canals; and with them also was Ea. In those days the world teemed,
the people multiplied, the world bellowed like a wild bull, and the
great god was aroused by the clamour. Enlil heard the clamour and
he said to the gods in council, 'The uproar of mankind is intolerable
and sleep is no longer possible by reason of the babel.' So the gods
agreed to exterminate mankind. Enlil did this, but Ea because of

his oath warned me in a dream. He whispered their words to my house of reeds, 'Reed-house, reed-house! Wall, O wall, hearken reed-house, wall reflect; O man of Shurrupak, son of Ubara-Tutu; tear down your house and build a boat, abandon possessions and look for life, despise worldly goods and save your soul alive. Tear down your house, I say, and build a boat. These are the measurements of the barque as you shall build her: let her beam equal her length, let her deck be roofed like the vault that covers the abyss; then take up into the boat the seed of all living creatures.'

When I had understood I said to my lord, 'Behold, what you have commanded I will honour and perform, but how shall I answer the people, the city, the elders?' Then Ea opened his mouth and said to me, his servant, 'Tell them this: I have learnt that Enlil is wrathful against me, I dare no longer walk in his land nor live in his city; I will go down to the Gulf to dwell with Ea my lord. But on you he will rain down abundance, rare fish and shy wild-fowl, a rich harvest-tide. In the evening the rider of the storm will bring you wheat in torrents.'

In the first light of dawn all my household gathered round me, the children brought pitch and the men whatever was necessary. On the fifth day I laid the keel and the ribs, then I made fast the planking. The ground-space was one acre, each side of the deck measured one hundred and twenty cubits, making a square. I built six decks below, seven in all, I divided them into nine sections with bulkheads between. I drove in wedges where needed, I saw to the punt-holes, and laid in supplies. The carriers brought oil in baskets, I poured pitch into the furnace and asphalt and oil; more oil was consumed in caulking, and more again the master of the boat took into his stores. I slaughtered bullocks for the people and every day I killed sheep. I gave the shipwrights wine to drink as though it were river water, raw wine and red wine and oil and white wine. There was feasting then as there is at the time of the New Year's festival; I myself anointed my head. On the seventh day the boat was complete.

Then was the launching full of difficulty; there was shifting of ballast above and below till two-thirds was submerged. I loaded into her all that I had of gold and of living things, my family, my kin, the beasts of the field both wild and tame, and all the craftsmen. I sent them on board, for the time that Shamash had ordained was already fulfilled when he said, 'In the evening, when the rider of the storm sends down the destroying rain, enter the boat and batten her down.' The time was fulfilled, the evening came, the rider of the storm sent down the rain. I looked out at the weather and it was terrible, so I too boarded the boat and battened her down. All was now complete, the battening and the caulking; so I handed the tiller to Puzur-Amurri the steersman, with the navigation and the care of the whole boat.

With the first light of dawn a black cloud came from the horizon; it thundered within where Adad, lord of the storm was riding. In front over hill and plain Shullat and Hanish, heralds of the storm, led on. Then the gods of the abyss rose up; Nergal pulled out the dams of the nether waters, Ninurta the warlord threw down the dykes, and the seven judges of hell, the Annunaki, raised their torches, lighting the land with their livid flame. A stupor of despair went up to heaven when the god of the storm turned daylight to darkness, when he smashed the land like a cup. One whole day the tempest raged, gathering fury as it went, it poured over the people like the tides of battle; a man could not see his brother nor the people to be seen from heaven. Even the gods were terrified at the flood, they fled to the highest heaven, the firmament of Anu; they crouched against the walls, cowering like curs. Then Ishtar the sweet-voiced Queen of Heaven cried out like a woman in travail: 'Alas, the days of old are turned to dust because I commanded evil; why did I command this evil in the council of all the gods? I commanded wars to destroy the people, but are they not my people, for I brought them forth? Now like the spawn of fish they float in the ocean.' The great gods of heaven and of hell wept, they covered their mouths.

For six days and six nights the winds blew, torrent and tempest and flood overwhelmed the world, tempest and flood raged together like warring hosts. When the seventh day dawned the storm from the south subsided, the sea grew calm, the flood was stilled; I looked at the face of the world and there was silence, all mankind was turned to clay. The surface of the sea stretched as flat as a rooftop; I opened a hatch and the light fell on my face. Then I bowed low, I sat down and I wept, the tears streamed down my face, for on every side was the waste of water. I looked for land in vain, but fourteen leagues distant there appeared a mountain, and there the boat grounded; on the mountain of Nisir the boat held fast, she held fast and did not budge. One day she held, and a second day on the mountain of Nisir she held fast and did not budge. A third day, and fourth day she held fast on the mountain and did not budge; a fifth day and a sixth day she held fast on the mountain. When the seventh day dawned I loosed a dove and let her go. She flew away, but finding no resting-place she returned. Then I loosed a swallow, and she flew away but finding no resting-place she returned. I loosed a raven, she saw that the waters had retreated, she ate, she flew around, she cawed, and she did not come back. Then I threw everything open to the four winds, I made a sacrifice and poured out a libation on the mountain top. Seven and again seven cauldrons I set up on their stands, I heaped up wood and cane and cedar and myrtle. When the gods smelled the sweet savour, they gathered like flies over the sacrifice. Then, at last, Ishtar also came, she lifted her necklace with the jewels of heaven that once Anu had made to please her. 'O you gods here present, by the lapis lazuli round my neck I shall remember these days as I remember the jewels of my throat; these last days I shall not forget. Let all the gods gather round the sacrifice, except Enlil. He shall not approach this offering, for without reflection he brought the flood; he consigned my people to destruction.'

When Enlil had come, when he saw the boat, he was wrath and swelled with anger at the gods, the host of heaven. 'Has any of these mortals escaped? Not one was to have survived the destruction.' Then the god of the wells and canals Ninurta opened his mouth and said to the warrior Enlil, 'Who is there of the gods that can devise without Ea? It is Ea alone who knows all things.' Then Ea opened his mouth and spoke to warrior Enlil, 'Wisest of gods, hero Enlil, how could you so senselessly bring down the flood?

> Lay upon the sinner his sin,
> Lay upon the transgressor his transgression,
> Punish him a little when he breaks loose,

Do not drive him too hard or he perishes;
Would that a lion had ravaged mankind
Rather than the flood,
Would that a wolf had ravaged mankind
Rather than the flood,
Would that famine had wasted the world
Rather than the flood,
Would that pestilence had wasted mankind
Rather than the flood.

It was not I that revealed the secret of the gods; the wise man learned it in a dream. Now take your counsel what shall be done with him.'

Then Enlil went up into the boat, he took me by the hand and my wife and made us enter the boat and kneel down on either side, he standing between us. He touched our foreheads to bless us saying, 'In time past Utnapishtim was a mortal man; henceforth he and his wife shall live in the distance at the mouth of the rivers.' Thus it was that the gods took me and placed me here to live in the distance, at the mouth of the rivers.

BABYLONIAN

¶ Bhagwan had created out of earth two washermen, male and female. From this brother and sister the human race had its birth. They lived happily and were very charitable. It fell to the girl's lot to draw water and when going to the river she would take rice with her to feed the fish. This went on for a long time.

Then one day the fish Ro asked her: 'Maiden, what reward do you desire? Have you thought of any definite thing?' She answered: 'I know of nothing.' Then the fish said: 'Through water the earth will be turned upside down. Take pumpkin seeds with you and make a cage. Then you and your brother step into the cage, taking seed and water with you. And do not forget to bring a cock also.'

The rains began to fall, slowly at first, then in ever greater torrents. It was as if earth and heaven had merged into one. Then God spoke: 'Thus have I turned the world upside down. But has not someone survived? The crowing of the cock informs me of it.'

50   Flood

Then Bhagwan himself went to find out more about the matter. He came to where the cage was and asked: 'Is anyone inside?' Then the girl answered: 'We are two inside, my brother and I.' And Bhagwan found within the cage two young people in the full prime and strength of life. Then God spoke: 'I have destroyed the whole world. Who warned you and gave you the advice to make such a cage? You must explain this mystery to me. For my plan was hidden from men.' Then the girl replied: 'It was the fish who instructed me.' Bhagwan then called the fish and asked: 'Was it you who brought the knowledge to these two?' The fish answered: 'Oh no, Lord Father, it was not I who did so.' Then God beat the fish and it became disposed to confess: 'Yes, Lord Father, I did really do it.' Then God spoke: 'Had you at once told the truth, nothing would have happened to you.' And God cut out the fish's tongue and threw it away. From this tongue leeches took their origin. But the fish has remained without tongue from that time till now.

God turned the girl with her face to the West and the young man with his face to the East. When he had made them turn again so as to face each other, he asked the man: 'Who is this?' and he answered: 'She is my wife.' Then Bhagwan asked the girl: 'Who is this?' and she answered: 'He is my husband.' Then God made them man and wife. In this way they became the progenitors of the human race. Generation followed generation and the different languages came into being.

INDIA *Bhil*

¶ There were two high mountains, and they argued and argued together which was the higher. God listened and in time grew tired of it. He said to them, 'I can cover both of you and then what does it matter which of you is higher?' But the mountains turned their backs on him and went on arguing. 'I warned you,' said God angrily, 'now look at this,' and he took out a golden comb and threw it mightily, right into the waves of the sea. It fell into the deepest part and when it reached the bottom turned into a golden crab which grew so big that in time its wide shell and huge claws stopped up the sea and made it overflow its shores. At the same time God split open the heavens and sent a great rain. The water from above and the water from below joined and were mighty, they became mightier by the minute, they rose and rose until everything was covered, the two high mountains were covered and as God had said it made no difference then which of them was higher. Nothing remained uncovered except for three other still higher mountains a long way away. All the peoples and animals on earth fled towards them but only those able to climb one of the three before the waters engulfed them were saved. The rest of the people in the world were drowned.

INDONESIA Nias

¶ Many years ago we lived not here upon this earth but down under the ground. And there came a time when we had no fruit and there was nothing to eat. So we sent the humming-bird to see what he could find. Wherever he might find fruit or food of any kind, there the people would go. He flew up into the sky, and there he saw a grape-vine that had its roots in the underworld and grew up through a hole in the middle of the sky into the upper world. The humming-bird saw the hole in the sky and flew through it, and came to a land where mescal and fruits and flowers of all kinds were growing. It was a good land. It was this world.

So the humming-bird flew back and told the people that he had seen a beautiful country above. 'Let us all go up there,' he said. So they all went up, climbing on the grape-vine. They climbed without stopping until they had come out through the hole in the sky into the upper world. But they left behind them in the underworld the frog-folk, who were blind. Now when the people had lived for a while in that land they heard a noise, and they wondered at it and sent a man to look down the hole through which they had come, to see what made the noise. The man looked and saw that waters were rising from the underworld and were already so high that they nearly reached the mouth of the hole. The people said, 'The blind frogs below have made this flood, and if it rises out of the hole it will wash us all away.' So they took counsel together, and then they hollowed out a tree like a trough and put into it plenty of fruits and blankets. They chose a beautiful maiden and laid her in the trough, and closed it up and said, 'Now if the waters come and we are all washed away, she will be saved alive.'

The flood came up through the hole, and the people ran to the mountains, but though the mountains were high the waters rose over them.

The trough floated like a boat, and the flood kept rising, till at last it nearly touched the sky. Still the waters rose till the waves dashed the trough against the sky, where it struck with a loud noise. It struck first to the south, then to the west, then to the north, then nearly to the east. Then the flood began to go down.

The people had said to the woman, 'If you hear the waters going down, wait till the trough rests on the earth, then make a little opening and look around you.'

When the trough rested on the ground the woman opened it and went out. She looked all around her over all the world, but saw no one. All the people had been drowned. Then the woman thought, 'How can I bear children and make a new people.'

She went up into the mountains early before sunrise, and lay there alone. Then the daylight came and the beams from the sun shone warm upon the woman, and the water dripped from the crag, and in this way she conceived, and bore a daughter. When the child was grown to maidenhood the mother said to her, 'Do you know, my daughter, how you came to be?' And the maid said, 'No.'

'I will show you,' said the mother.

So she led her daughter up into the mountains, and bade her lie down as she herself had lain. And the maid lay on the mountain all day. Next morning early, before sunrise, the mother went to her, and she lay down upon her daughter and looked at the sun. Then she quickly sprang up, and in this way the maiden conceived of the sun, and the child that she bore was the Son of God – Sekala Ka-amja, 'The-One-Who-Never-Died.'

NORTH AMERICA *Mojave Apache*

¶ There was once a husband and wife called Kitimil and Magigi. But Magigi had a father whose name was Insatiable, and whose appetite was so enormous that nothing could satisfy it. He kept on eating and he kept on growing until he had eaten every coconut on the island and a good deal else besides, and until he was so big he filled the large assembly house and still part of him poked out on top and from either side. They grew sugar cane in that place as well as coconuts. One day Kitimil went out to look at this field and found the cane all nibbled as if some small animal had been eating it. But when he went home and told his wife there was a mouse in the sugar-cane field she said:

'That means my father must still be hungry.'

'But what can one so large have to do with one so small?'

'Surely you know my father can turn himself into a mouse,' said Magigi.

Kitimil did not believe her. He went away and made a mousetrap; that evening he set it in the sugar-cane fields, and finding a dead mouse in it the next morning he was very pleased with himself. His wife turned pale.

'You have killed my father,' she said. 'Now what will become of us?'

'Nonsense,' said Kitimil, but when he went to look for his father-in-law sure enough he was nowhere to be found.

'Leave me alone,' said Magigi. 'I have to think what we should do.'

In the morning she told Kitimil, 'Take four teeth from the mouse and all of its blood. Then bury it. Then come back to me, but don't delay because a great storm is going to come and the seas are going to rise and we've got to get away from here as fast as possible.' When Kitimil returned she gave him some leaves and some oil to take together with the mouse's blood and its teeth, and she walked with him to the top of the highest mountain.

'Now,' she said, 'we have to build a pile house with seven storeys.' So they worked and worked for seven days, and each day they built a new storey to their pile house. On the seventh day the great storm broke and the sea rose from its bed and began to cover the whole island.

When it reached the top of the mountain Kitimil and Magigi gathered up the teeth and the blood and the leaves and the oil and climbed into the first storey of their house. The next day, the flood continuing to rise, they climbed into the second storey and so on each day until on the seventh day they had climbed into the seventh and last storey of their pile house. And still the flood rose all round them. Then Magigi took the teeth and the blood and she threw them out upon the flood. She put oil upon a leaf and laid it on the water at her feet. At once the waters ceased to rise; in a little while too the rain stopped falling, the thunder and lightning stopped flashing and banging and the waters began to go down again. After seven days the whole land was dry.

But when Kitimil and Magigi came down from their mountain they found themselves the only people left alive, except for one man who by lashing himself to the outrigger of his canoe and anchoring the canoe to a particularly large stone had managed to save himself. They all went home together. In time Magigi gave birth to seven children, she set them in each part of the island and so there were people there again.

MELANESIA, CAROLINE ISLANDS

¶ Once a group of men went fishing in a deep lake. They baited their hooks with meat and put out their lines. One man almost immediately felt a huge tug on his and when he looked into the water to see what he had caught realised very quickly that he had hooked a bunyip.

'Unhook it,' said his fellows. 'Let it go. There'll be a disaster if you don't.'

'No,' said the man, 'I won't.' He dragged the bunyip to the shore and took it away with him. But the bunyip's mother had also lived in the lake. When she discovered she had lost her son she said to the waters, 'You must follow that man.' At once they rose higher and higher till they covered every bit of the country – all the people fled to the highest mountains but quite in vain for the waters followed them even there, rising up and up the mountain until it lapped about their feet, at which every one of them turned into a black swan and has remained a black swan to this day.

AUSTRALIA, VICTORIA

¶ Once a great flood occurred and the sea rose and overflowed the earth, the hills being covered and people and animals hurrying to the top of Tauaga, the highest mountain. But the sea followed and all were afraid. Yet the king of the snakes, Raudalo, did not fear. At last he said to the servants, 'Where now are the waters?' And they answered, 'They are rising, lord.' Yet he would not look upon the flood. And after a space he said again, 'Where now are the waters?' and his servants answered as they had done before. Once again he inquired of them, 'Where now are the waters?' But this time all the snakes, Titiko, Dubo and Anaur, made answer, 'They are here and in a moment they will touch you, lord.'

Then Raudalo turned about and put out his forked tongue and with the tip of it touched the angry waters which were about to cover him. And suddenly the sea rose no more, but began to flow down the side of the mountain. Still Raudalo was not content, and he pursued the flood down the hill, all the time putting out his forked tongue so that the waters would not delay. Thus they went down the mountain and over the plain country until the seashore was reached. And the waters lay in their bed once more and the flood was stayed.

NEW GUINEA, PAPUA

The Best and Worst Nail in the Ark
¶ The shipwright who made the Ark left empty a place for a nail in it, because he was sure that he himself would not be taken into it. When Noah went into the Ark with his children, as the angel had told him, Noah shut the windows of the Ark and raised his hand to bless it. Now the Devil had come into the Ark along with him as he went into it, and when Noah blessed the Ark the Devil found no

other way but the empty hole which the shipwright had left unclosed, and he went into it in the form of a snake; and because of the tightness of the hole he could not go out nor come back, and he was like this until the Flood ebbed; and that is the best and the worst nail that was in the Ark.

IRELAND

¶ Divine Yao was a perfect monarch and a model sage, polite, intelligent, accomplished and thoughtful, besides extremely obliging. His merit was felt in every part of the land and among every class of people. Yet although the result of it was universal peace, still all was not well during his reign, for the land suffered from a spate of floods and no one seemed able to repair them. The Minister of Works in whose responsibility it lay achieved precisely nothing when he attempted it. 'Alas,' said the Divine Yao; 'this man is worthy of respect only in appearance. Look! The floods embrace the hills, threaten the heaven even, all the lower people groan and murmur. Is there no one competent who can correct this calamity for me?'

'How about Kun?' suggested his courtiers.

'That fellow is perverse,' said Yao. 'He tries to get the better of his peers.'

'There is no one else. You had better try him.'

So Yao sent for Kun and Kun laboured for nine years, but to no avail. About this time Yao said, 'I have been seventy years on my throne. It is time another succeeded me.' So he set out to find a virtuous successor and settled finally on one Shun, a man of lowly family, whose virtue he had tested by every means possible, even sending him into a forest at the foot of the wild hills, but no sound or storm could make him go astray. Wherever Shun went he created harmony where before had been disorder, among farmers and fishermen and craftsmen alike.

So in time Shun became emperor. He administered the land and the law quite fairly and well, visiting all the feudal lords and investigating their works, setting standards of measurement and instituting

Flood   57

penal codes. He was also most bountiful. Yet his chief problem still was flood. Kun had not only failed to stem it, he had actually made it worse. For he had tried to dam the water and thus confused all the five elements. The Lord of Heaven was so angry at this he had refused to give him the great plan with its nine divisions. Kun was imprisoned then and his son Yu rose and assumed his task.

Yu had a long neck, a mouth like a raven's beak and his face was hideous. Yet to him the Lord of Heaven gave the great plan with its nine divisions, where the unchanging principles of its method were in due order set forth. For Yu did not try to dam the waters, instead he dug the courses of streams and of the great rivers, the Hsiang, the Huai, the Ho and Han; he drove out all the snakes and dragons so that the people were able to settle down on the land unmolested. Then he hewed down trees of the hills, showed the people how to catch fish and birds and beasts for food, and together with the Minister of Agriculture showed them how to sow grain. He taught them the bartering of goods, thus to get what they needed in exchange for what they had too much of. Gradually the once flooded land and all its regions came under good rule.

For ten years Yu worked and planned without seeing his own home. He grew neither nails on his hands nor hair on his head and contracted an illness that shrivelled up half his body. Whenever people saw others walking the way he walked they called it 'the walk of Yu'. But they blessed him for what he had done.

'Were it not for Yu,' they said, 'we must all surely have become fishes.'

CHINESE

¶ The gods were displeased with the Indians because they fought and killed each other, even little children were killed sometimes with arrows. Venus had taken a man's shape and lived on earth in those days; he was not a pleasant sight, covered all over with open sores. And the sores stank. When he came to some villages the people would hold their noses and run away from him, and if he came to their houses to ask for help they would slam the door in his face and not let him in.

Only one man took pity on him. 'You are welcome,' he said, leading Venus over his threshold. He sat him down on a new mat on the floor and summoned his daughter to bring a bowl of clean water and to wash his sores. Afterwards he ordered her to sit on Venus' lap and to hug and caress and comfort him.

Next day Venus said to the man, 'What do you want? The God is angry with the Indians because they kill each other. Do you want to live or die?'

'I'd rather live of course,' the man said. 'But why are you asking?'

'I have been an unworthy guest. You brought me in though I stank and no-one else wanted me. And now your house is full of the rankness of my wounds. You ordered your daughter to be kind to me and I took advantage of that, I dishonoured her. What will she do now? What man will marry her? You'd have every right to throw me from your door.'

'You are still my honoured guest,' the man replied gravely. And he saw Venus on his way with the utmost politeness. Before he was taken up by a whirlwind, Venus said, 'Catch yourself a pigeon and take it to your house.'

The man could not think why Venus had told him this. Nevertheless he loosed his arrow at a passing pigeon and when it fell to earth picked up the carcase and carried it home.

Next day the rain began to fall. It fell and fell and the river rose and rose. And as the rain fell and the river rose so the pigeon's carcase grew and grew until it had turned into a large boat. The man and his family climbed into it, they floated safely on the water, and stayed there, floating, till the flood went down, though all the other Indians had been swept away by then and drowned.

SOUTH AMERICA *Sherente*

¶ Noj was a good man at a time when every other man was bad; or so God thought. At any rate he had decided to drown the lot of them, all except Noj, whom he warned in a whisper, 'Build a boat, Noj, build a boat.' And since Noj was accustomed to obeying the word of God, so he did, going deep into the forest each day and building it secretly from the best timbers. The only other person who knew about it was his wife.

The Devil grew very curious. He sidled up to Noj's wife one morning and said, 'Do me a favour, lady, tell me just what that man of yours is up to.'

'Certainly not,' said Noj's wife virtuously. 'It's between him and me and God, and has nothing whatever to do with you.'

'Suppose,' said the Devil, 'I were to offer you . . .'

'And whatever can you offer me, you ugly little runt?'

'A sweet tongue,' said the Devil, 'for a start; or beauty, or anything you like, a lighter hand with the baking, a speedier hand on the spindle; if only you tell me what Noj is making in the forest.'

'If I did,' said Noj's wife, 'I can't see you providing them.'

'Well then, wouldn't you like to know why Noj is doing whatever he is doing in the forest? Did he tell you that? Don't say you haven't been a little anxious.'

'I did wonder, that is the truth,' said Noj's wife, 'I hope he's not crazy, but . . .'

'So what harm can there be in it?'

Noj's wife sighed. 'Would you promise to tell me anything you find out?'

'Cross my heart, lady, and hope to die,' the Devil said.

So Noj's wife told the Devil that Noj was building a boat. And the Devil looked wise and went away and when he came back a few hours later told her that God was planning to send them on a long sea voyage, but he couldn't tell her why because even Noj didn't know that yet.

'But how's he going to get the boat from the forest to the river,' asked Noj's wife in astonishment.

'Perhaps he could do with some advice from me,' said the Devil and went away again. But from that time on, while Noj continued to build his boat by day, at night, secretly, the Devil crept in and undid his work, pulling out nails and breaking up timbers; thus each morning Noj had to begin work all over again.

'There's a jinx on me,' said Noj, crossly. 'At this rate I'll never get it done before the flood comes.' He worked harder and harder but all to no avail, and every day the skies grew heavier. Noj prayed to God then, but God was too busy preparing for the flood to take any notice of the Devil's activities (indeed he did not think he needed to, now that he planned to wipe out all the Devil's disciples). Nor did he hear Noj's prayer; until one day, at last, great drops of rain began to fall. Noj laid down his hammer and his saw and got down on his knees and prayed to God harder than ever.

'It's much too soon, God, my boat is not nearly finished, through no fault of mine. In fact I was beginning to think you didn't want me to finish it. Yet you promised to save us, oh help me, God.' At that moment Noj's wife appeared with all her children clinging to her skirts and all her chickens and cows and pigs and sheep behind.

'I thought your boat could save us, husband, but whatever kind of boat is this,' she said. For the boat had only ribs and framework still, it had no planking, let alone a cabin with a roof, made of stout timbers caulked with pitch as Noj had planned it. 'Oh woe, oh woe, we'll all be drowned,' cried she.

From beyond the forest her cries were echoed as the waters rose; men climbed to the tops of their houses and clung to them helplessly, lashed by rain and wind. They took their animals with them if they could, all the rest were left floating on the tide. Noj and his family dragged themselves and their animals up the framework of his boat until they reached the highest point. But the waters went on rising all the time. And now dead people came floating past besides dead animals.

'Oh God,' prayed Noj, 'I am a virtuous man and why did you tell me to build my boat if you did not want me saved?'

'Oh God,' prayed Noj's wife, 'why did you ever let me have anything to do with the Devil?'

The water was already about their feet. But now something else moved gently towards them – 'Like a *boat*,' cried one of the children. 'It *is* a boat,' another said. It struck the timbers of Noj's unfinished boat with a dull clang and waited while they all scrambled down to it. But they did not find wood beneath their feet this time. When they bent down and touched the deck their hands met something cool and smooth and hard, that glimmered faintly in the dying light, that was the same colour as the rain itself. 'This boat is made of iron,' said Noj. 'God has sent it to us surely. There never was such a miracle.'

'Better than a lighter hand with the baking or speedier hand with the spindle any day,' said his wife. But Noj did not know what she was talking about.

So it was that Noj and his wife and their children, their chickens and cows and pigs and sheep were saved from the flood that engulfed all the rest of mankind. They floated away on their iron boat while the thunder boomed and the lightning flashed and the rain fell unceasingly. In the end there was no land to be seen at all.

And if when the flood subsided they were the only people left upon earth, nonetheless there they were and it wasn't wholly the Devil's to do what he liked with. One thing was certain, Noj's wife would never listen to that voice again: though one can't say the same of all her descendents.

RUSSIA, SIBERIA

FIRE

As for the Earth, out of it cometh bread:
and under it is turned up as it were fire.
                              The Book of Job

Fires inwrap the earthly globe, yet man is not
consum'd; . . .
                              William Blake

Fire, according to the anthropologist Claude Lévi-Strauss, is what transforms natural man into cultured man. Not till he owns the means of warming himself and, more important still, of cooking his food can he properly be distinguished from the animal. It is a materialist view, perhaps, strictly speaking, but sensible. In all events the stress put on the acquisition of fire, mythologically, indicates its importance for most people. Usually regarded as magic (no mystery in that, you only have to look at fire still, now) it is therefore invariably regarded as having been the special property of some god or at the least of a superior being. He/she, moreover, for one reason or another, because he does not want to lose power and/or because he is angry with men, or because he fears the consequence of such knowledge, is very often unwilling to share it. Thus fire, whether the thing itself or the secret of its making ('Take the sharpness of stone and the hardness of iron ...' as the Siberian story says) has to be tricked out of him, something done very often by that mysterious figure known to so many cultures, the trickster. A figure neither man nor god, nor good nor bad, the trickster's prototype in Western culture is the Titan, Prometheus.

It is apt enough. For fire too, just like the trickster, is morally neutral. It is not only the source of life, but also, being dangerous and unpredictable, the source of death. It not only burns or warms the wicked, but also, as readily, burns or warms the good. Furthermore, because it leads man one step beyond his natural animal limits it has to be paid for, much as Icarus paid for going too near the sun, Dr Faustus for his worldly knowledge, Marie Curie for studying radium – and all of us, perhaps, for the benefits of nuclear power. Some of the payment demanded in the fire myths is minor enough: the deer's blackened tail; the robin's red breast; or, as here, the gadfly's licence to feed for ever on the 'calves of the gentle and simple'. But much more common, beginning with the Prometheus myth and its sequel – the story in which Pandora looses disease and pain and misery on the waiting world – in myth after myth the price of the acquisition of fire is, precisely, death.

¶ Aidne, son of Allguba, son of Eithrel – he was the first man to kindle a campfire for the sons of Mil: it was easy for him, he needed only to wring his two hands, whereupon the flashes of fire poured out of his knuckles as large as fresh, wild apples when their harvesting begins.

IRELAND

¶ There was a great flood once and only two saved, a boy and a girl who floated on the water in a gourd. Afterwards they had seven sons, but none of them had fire to cook their food because it had all been extinguished in the flood. At last the brothers held a council and decided to send a messenger to the sky to ask its spirit if he would give them fire once more. The eldest brother volunteered to go himself. And when he reached the sky the spirit granted his request quite willingly. But he had barely reached the gate of the spirit's palace before the torch that he had lit went out. So he returned a second time to relight it, and again the same thing happened. He made yet a third attempt; but though this time he succeeded in carrying the flaming torch more than halfway back to earth, a gust of wind suddenly extinguished it, and thus it was he arrived home fireless.

The brothers conferred once more. After much argument they chose the owl and the serpent to be their messengers, and the owl and the serpent set out on the journey to heaven. Unfortunately the first village they came to was infested with rats – the moment the owl fell to hunting them he forgot his errand completely, and while the serpent went on a little way alone, as soon as he reached the marsh the croak of the tree-frogs distracted him, he began to chase them hither and thither. So owl hunts rats and the serpent chases tree-frogs right to this very day. But neither of them has ever succeeded in reaching heaven.

The brothers took council for a third time. At the end of it they decided to ask the gadfly to help them: 'Willingly,' said the gadfly, 'but I'll want a reward for my pains. If I bring you fire you must promise that I and my children and my children's children will have the right to quench our thirst for ever on the thighs of the buffalo and the calves of the gentle and simple.' The brothers agreed it would be so. So off went the gadfly and knocked on the gate of heaven. And when it was opened he asked the spirit very nicely for some fire to take home with him – 'Certainly,' said the spirit of the sky. 'But you must hide your eyes while I kindle it, you cannot have the secret of my kindling. Where do you keep your eyes, incidentally? And where do you keep your ears?'

'My eyes,' said the gadfly, 'I keep where your ears are. My ears I keep where you have your two eyes. So if you put a pitcher over my head I would see right throught it. On the other hand if you cover me by a basket with interstices then I will not see anything at all.'

The sky spirit believed him, every word he said. He put the basket over the gadfly and began to kindle his fire at once while the gadfly watched his every action closely. Afterwards the gadfly took a torch and lit it just as the eldest brother had done and set off back to earth. Of course the fire went out before he was halfway home but why should the gadfly mind, he knew all its secrets.

'Where is the fire?' asked the brothers anxiously when he arrived home fireless: 'Where have you put the fire?'

'Nowhere,' answered the gadfly, 'except in your making. Now listen to me carefully. Take a splinter of wood as narrow as the leg of a roebuck and fine as the beard of a shrimp. Make a notch in it, set a cord in the notch and pile tow all round like a nest of little pigs. Then pull the cord strongly back and forth until the smoke rises and the tow begins to burn.'

All this the brothers did. They had fire in no time at all, and ever since have been able to cook their victuals. As for the gadfly, he too had won his comfort; to this day he and his children and children's children have drunk from the thighs of the buffalo and the calves of the gentle and simple.

THAILAND

¶ Kudai had created earth and everything upon earth. He had created man to live on it and enjoy its fruits. But the cold was too strong. In the winter snow and ice ruled everything and man was naked and he shivered. Kudai said, 'How shall man live naked in the snow and ice? I must discover fire to him or he will die.'

The man was called Ulgen and he had three daughters, young, pretty and frivolous. When Kudai came to earth to visit them the girls saw him coming along the road but did not know who he was, this bent old man with a long beard; so immediately they began to giggle. 'How comical he looks,' they said. When the beard got in the way of Kudai's feet and he tripped and almost fell, they laughed so much they nearly died of laughing.

He looked at them. He stilled them with his look. He said, 'Enjoy your mockery. You will regret it after. The gift I was bringing I will take away again and you will weep, you will curse me for its lack.' He left them and went on along the road, while the three daughters of Ulgen stared at each other anxiously. The youngest then set off after him, the other two following without a word. They trod very quietly. Kudai was still muttering to himself so angrily that he did not hear them come and the closer they got to him the more quietly they trod. At last when he stopped and sat down against a rock to rest they hid themselves behind the rock. Kudai went on muttering, muttering, soon they were able to pick out words here and there and then whole sentences. 'Fire' they heard, and 'Warmth' and 'Light' – they looked at each other, shivering, and listened still harder. 'They shall go without,' they heard: and then a laugh, a little laugh, so small it might have sounded only in their heads; yet, too, was like a thunder in the heavens. 'They will never find it now,' they heard. 'The sharpness of stone; the hardness of iron. They will never find it now.'

The sharpness of stone; the hardness of iron. They went home wondering, repeating the words to themselves. And found their father still trying to kindle fire vainly, using a birch twig and a stone together.

'Try the sharpness of stone with the hardness of iron,' they said as they watched him.

'Why do you say that, my daughters?'

'Kudai the creator said it to himself; we were hidden and we heard it.'

Ulgen took a knife made of iron; he took a stone. He struck them together, and at once between the sharpness of the one and the hardness of the other a spark sprang out. He struck them together again and this time he put his birch twig to the spark and a flame was kindled. From that time on there was fire in the homes of man; through sharpness of stone and hardness of iron Ulgen and his daughters were able to warm themselves.

RUSSIA, SIBERIA

¶ Once only the God had fire and the pygmies went without. God's mother was old and her bones ached and she sat warming herself by the fire all day, but God did not stay at home with her, because he had a swing made out of lianas and he would spend his time swinging from tree to tree and from one river to another. But one day when the God came home he found his mother weeping, shivering and fireless, for a pygmy had come and stolen the fire while she was asleep. 'If you don't fetch me back my fire I shall die for cold,' she said. So God went to the pygmy village and took the fire and returned home to his mother.

But a second pygmy came. Again God returned home to find his mother fireless. And a second time he set off to where the pygmies lived to fetch his fire for her. Immediately a third pygmy determined to steal it. But he was cleverer than most. He caught a bird and plucked the feathers from it and made himself a pair of wings. Then he flew to God's village and picked up the fire and flew away with it. The God's mother awoke at once this time, she bawled and cried until her son came flying in on his swing made of lianas.

'Stop the thief; run after him; before I start shivering again.' So off went God chasing the pygmy, chasing him over the hills and down into the very depths. But he could not catch him. At last he called out, 'You are my equal and my brother now,' and went home to his village, only to find his mother lying dead there from the cold. The God wept. He called to the pygmies,

'You are my equals now. But you will be my equal in all things. As my mother has died, so shall you die, from now and for ever and ever.' And so it has been; from that time not only have men warmed themselves by the fire and cooked their food on it, but also at their lives' end they have died, as God's mother did in the ancient time.

AFRICA

¶ Once only Chief Woodpecker of the wolves had fire, though all the tribes of people needed it. When the wolves' winter ceremony was drawing near the chief of the rival tribe gathered his warriors together and asked which of them was brave enough to try to steal it. 'I am,' said Deer. So the chief gave him some hair-oil in a seaweed bottle, a comb and a piece of stone and told Deer to keep them carefully until he needed them. 'And if you are still in trouble then,' he said, 'you can give the fire to the periwinkle, for it will, quite certainly, be safe with him.'

Next the chief fixed stones to protect Deer's feet: Woodpecker had set sharp sticks into the floor of his house, he said, to discourage anyone who tried to rob him. And finally he tied cedar bark to Deer's elbows. 'First you must dance round the fire,' he told him, 'as close, as close as you are able. But soon you must say it is too hot for you and ask for the smoke-hole to be opened. And then suddenly as you dance for the second time, you must spring and bend your elbows to the fire, spring a second time right out of the smoke-hole, and run because the wolves will undoubtedly be after you at once.'

So the chief and the people and the Deer all came to the wolves' house for the winter ceremony, and the Deer danced alone in front of it. Woodpecker's daughter said, 'Let Deer dance in our house, for he seems to me to dance particularly well.'

Her father said, 'All right. Open the doors, invite them in. But watch carefully and do not let Deer dance too near the fire. And make sure you bolt the doors behind him.'

So all the people entered the house and the doors were tightly bolted and Deer began to dance again. But he danced quite slowly now as if he was feeling very weak. And soon he said,

'This house is much too hot for dancing. You must open the smoke-hole widely so that the air can blow in and cool me.' The wolves looked up at the smoke-hole and decided it was too high for even nimble Deer to reach, so they opened it. And the people began to sing again and Deer to dance, this time much more energetically. But all the time he danced nearer to the fire until Woodpecker sent a warrior to warn him away from it. And at once Deer jumped mightily almost into the fire itself, the sparks flew up and his cedar-bark elbows began to smoulder. He made a second leap even mightier, right up this time, out of the smoke-hole, out into the woods, and then he ran, faster and faster, fast as he could run. But the wolves ran faster still behind – Deer could already feel their breath on his back, when suddenly he remembered the Chief's three gifts. So he took out the stone and threw it down, immediately a high mountain stood in the middle of the path. Deer ran on for a while quite safely while the wolves were struggling to scale the mountain. He ran a long way. Yet then once more he heard the wolves come howling. He took out his gifts again, and this time he hurled the comb behind him, it grew immediately into a thorny wood. The wolves fought their way through it bit by bit. Deer ran and ran. He ran a long way. But at last the wolves had almost caught up with him again, so he took out the seaweed bottle and poured the hair-oil on the ground; and suddenly a great lake had divided the path, he was on one side of it, the wolves on the other. So they had to swim, while he ran on – ran and ran and ran and ran. He ran a long way. Until at last he saw Periwinkle sitting by the path and panted up to him and said,

'You'll have to keep the fire for me.' For the wolves had swum across the lake by now. He could hear them gaining on him in the distance.

He threw the fire into Periwinkle's mouth. And Periwinkle closed it very tightly. When the wolves came along and asked which way Deer had gone he could only grunt and gobble and wave his arms at them and the wolves did not know which way to run at all. So in the end they lost Deer's track entirely and had to go home empty-handed. Deer meanwhile gave fire to all the people and it belonged to everyone from that time forth, except for the wolves who lost it altogether; that's why perhaps wolves hate fire to this day.

¶ Ukko made fire again after the sun and the moon had been stolen from mankind. He struck the flaming sword against his finger-nail and gave the spark that jumped out to one of the Virgins of the air. But she let it escape from her fingers and the spark fell hissing through the clouds, fell down and down through the nine vaults and six lids of the air. Finally it fell into a lake and was swallowed by a blue trout much to its misery. For the spark burned so fiercely in its belly it swam to and fro across the lake forgetting all caution, quite soon a red salmon had come up and eaten it. But the spark burned in the belly of the salmon as it had burned in the belly of the trout, it too turned this way and that, trying to escape the pain, until it was snapped up by a grey pike, which suffering in its turn fell prey at last to the strong net woven by the hero Vainamoienen. Vainamoienen cut open the grey pike, then he cut open the red salmon he found inside it, then he cut open the blue trout he found inside that. And there lay the spark; but it jumped out and escaped him and set the whole countryside burning and burning. Vainamoienen pursued it as hard as he was able and before it had quite destroyed everything he managed to capture it, shutting it in a birch stump and a copper jar, from which men have been able to kindle it since and make fire to warm themselves.

FINLAND

¶ Long ago the great primordial hero Maui thought he would destroy the fires of his ancestress Mahu-ika. So he got up in the night, and put out the fires left in the cooking-houses of each family of the village; then, quite early in the morning, he called aloud to the servants, 'I hunger, I hunger; quick, cook some food for me.'

One of the servants thereupon ran as fast as he could to make up the fire to cook some food, but the fire was out; and as he ran round from house to house in the village to get a light, he found every fire quite out – he could nowhere get a light.

When Maui's mother heard this, she called out to the servants, and said, 'Some of you repair to my great ancestress Mahu-ika; tell her that fire has been lost upon earth, and ask her to give some to the world again.' But the slaves were alarmed and refused to obey her commands. At last Maui said to his mother, 'Well; then I will fetch down fire for the world; but which is the path by which I must go?' And his parents said to him, 'Follow that broad path that lies just before you there; and you will at last reach the dwelling of an ancestress of yours; and if she asks you who you are, you had better call out your name to her, then she will know you are a descendant of hers; but be cautious, and do not play any tricks with her, because we have heard that your deeds are greater than the deeds of men, and that you are fond of deceiving and injuring others, and perhaps you even now intend in many ways to deceive this old ancestress of yours, but pray be cautious not to do so.' And Maui answered, 'No, I only want to bring fire away for men, that is all, and I'll return again as soon as I can do that.'

Then he went and reached the abode of the goddess of fire; and he was so filled with wonder at what he saw, that for a long time he could say nothing. At last he said, 'Oh, lady, would you rise up? Where is your fire kept? I have come to beg some from you.' Then the aged lady rose right up, and said, 'Au-e! who can this mortal be?' and he answered, 'It is I.' 'Where do you come from?' said she, and he answered, 'I belong to this country.' 'You are not from this country,' said she; 'your appearance is not like that of the inhabitants of this country. Do you come from the north-east?' He replied, 'No.' 'Do you come from the south-east?' He replied, 'No.' 'Are you from the south?' He replied, 'No.' 'Are you from the westward?' He answered, 'No.' 'Come you, then, from the direction of the wind which blows right upon me?' and he said, 'I do.' 'Oh, then,' cried she, 'you are my grandchild; what do you want here?' He answered, 'I am come to beg fire from you.' She replied, 'Welcome, welcome; here then is fire for you.'

Then the aged woman pulled out her nail, and as she pulled it out fire flowed from it, and she gave it to him. And when Maui saw she had drawn out her nail to produce fire for him, he thought it a most wonderful thing! Then he went a short distance off and put the fire out, and returning to her said, 'The light you gave me has gone out, give me another.' Then she caught hold of another nail, and pulled it out as a light for him; and he left her, and went a little on one side, and put out that light also; then he went back to her again, and said, 'Oh, lady, give me, I pray you, another light, for the last one has also gone out.' And thus he went on and on until she had pulled out all the nails of the fingers of one of her hands; and then she began with the other hand, until she had pulled all the finger-nails out of that hand, too; and then she commenced upon the nails of her feet, and pulled them also out in the same manner, except the nail of one of her big toes. Then the aged woman said to herself at last, 'This fellow is surely playing tricks with me.'

Then out she pulled the one toe-nail that she had left, and it too became fire, and as she dashed it down on the ground the whole place caught fire. And she cried out to Maui, 'There, you have it all now!' And Maui ran off, and made a rush to escape, but the fire followed hard after him; so he changed himself into a fleet-winged eagle, and flew with rapid flight, but the fire pursued and almost caught him as he flew. Then the eagle dashed down into a pool of water, but he found the water almost boiling too. The forests also caught fire, so that the bird could not alight anywhere; and the earth and the sea both caught fire too, and Maui was very near perishing in the flames.

Then he called on his ancestors, Tawhiri-ma-tea and Whatitiri-matakataka, to send down an abundant supply of water, and he cried aloud, 'Oh, let water be given to me to quench this fire which pursues after me,' and lo, then appeared squalls and gales, and Tawhiri-ma-tea sent heavy lashing rain, and the fire was quenched; and before Mahu-ika could reach her place of shelter, she almost perished in the rain, and her shrieks and screams became as loud as those of Maui had been, when he was scorched by the pursuing fire: thus Maui ended this proceeding. In this manner was extinguished the fire of Mahu-ika, the goddess of fire; but before it was all lost, she saved a few sparks which she threw, to protect them, into the *kaiko-mako*, and a few other trees, where they are still cherished; hence, men yet use portions of the wood of these trees for fire when they require a light.

NEW ZEALAND *Maori*

¶ Once an Indian went hunting with his young brother-in-law Botoque. Near a tall cliff they noticed some macaws flying about and when they looked up saw the nest there. 'There'll be nestlings,' the elder man said. 'Climb up and get them, boy, and we'll have a treat tonight.' So Botoque climbed the cliff by a ladder his brother-in-law had made but found no nestlings in the nest, only two eggs. 'Take them; throw them down to me,' the man shouted to him. And Botoque threw them down. But these were magic eggs, they changed into stones while they were falling and hurt the man's hands quite badly. He thought Botoque had done it on purpose and in his fury he broke the ladder and left Botoque sitting on the cliff with no means of getting down to the ground again. 'May you starve; may you rot,' said the man as he went away.

For several days Botoque remained there alone. He grew thinner and thinner and hungrier and hungrier, for there was nothing in the nest but excrement, nor did the macaws return to it, though he expected them daily and was afraid because he had thrown down their eggs. One day however he saw a spotted jaguar out hunting, a bow and arrows slung across his back. The boy shrank back afraid, but the jaguar saw his shadow move across the ground below; he thought it some beast at first and tried to catch it, all in vain. Then he looked up and noticed the boy above him on the cliff and the broken ladder hanging down.

'I'll mend it for you,' he called up, and so he did, but Botoque was much too afraid at first to climb down it to meet him. In the end hunger and loneliness overcame the boy. When he had descended the ladder the jaguar put him on his back and carried him home to supper.

'It will be a good one too,' he said. 'Meat roasted on my fire, you'll have never tasted anything so good.' Botoque could not imagine what this roasted meat could be. Men had no fire in those days, so they did not know how to cook. And at first sight of the tree-trunk burning in a hearth made of stones, he could not imagine what he was seeing. The meat was delicious however, he ate and ate and ate, and when the jaguar offered to adopt him as his son he accepted gladly.

Unfortunately the jaguar was not alone in his village. He had a wife and she did not like Botoque at all. When her husband was away hunting she treated him very badly, scratching his face and giving him only dried-up remnants of meat to eat. The jaguar was angry and scolded her, but still she went on ill-treating the boy, sometimes feeding him nothing but leaves, and at last the jaguar said to Botoque,

'It is time you came hunting with me.' And once they were in the forest he gave the boy a new bow and arrows of his own and taught him how to use them as he did.

'Next time she ill-treats you, you have my permission to shoot an arrow into her,' he said.

The jaguar's wife would not heed any warnings. Next day she scratched Botoque's face again. So he shot an arrow into her breast and she fell down dead, and at once Botoque seized his bow and a piece of roasted meat and fled away back to his own village because he was afraid of the jaguar's anger.

No one recognised him there at first. Nor could Botoque make the other Indians believe his story. But then he offered them some of his roasted meat and as soon as they had tasted it they wanted to know how to cook meat for themselves.

'You need fire,' Botoque told them. 'Only the jaguar has fire.'

'Then we will have to take it away from him,' they said. Botoque showed the men the way to the jaguar's village and when they reached it they found no one at home and the meat raw, the jaguar's wife being dead. The Indians roasted the meat then and there and ate it, then they crept away from the village carrying the fire, and from that time on they had light to see by when night fell, they could warm themselves when it was cold and no longer must they eat their meat uncooked.

The jaguar on the other hand became their enemy for ever. Ever since men stole his weapon and his fire he has used only his claws for hunting, he rends his prey with his teeth as soon as he has caught it, eats it raw just as it is; and the only fire that remains to him is the fire that shines reflected in his eyes.

SOUTH AMERICA *Kayape Gorotive*

¶ The tiger said, 'Fire will come from my ear.' But the elephant said, 'No, fire will come from *my* ear.' In the end the gods gave fire to the crow and the crow gave it to men.

INDIA

Prometheus

¶ As for the legendary Prometheus: he was, to be sure, an oddity, the kind you might expect at the beginning of a world before the orders of things have entirely arranged themselves. He was not quite a god, but nor was he a man, springing from that breed of giants known as Titans, sons of the elements, fathers of the gods and ancestors of the human race. He was by far the most famous of them, except perhaps for his brother Atlas, the one whose fate it is to bear the heavens on his shoulders. Certainly he must have been the most cunning – Crooked Thought, they used to call him. Some even say it was Prometheus who created man, taking water and moulding him from clay, others say no and hint at different origins. Whatever the truth it is quite certain that Prometheus did favour men over gods, though he kept that to himself at first. Indeed when the other Titans made war on the gods he refused to support them, offered his services to great Zeus instead, and in return Zeus' daughter, the goddess Athene (at whose birth, fully-armed from Zeus' head Prometheus had assisted) taught him all the useful arts such as astronomy and architecture, medicine and mathematics; these in turn Prometheus passed on to men.

Fire   77

Zeus, unfortunately, did not approve of this. Watching the growing powers and skill of Prometheus' protegés, he began to see them as a challenge to himself. At one stage he determined to annihilate mankind entirely, and it was only by skilful argument that Prometheus dissuaded him. And still the more accomplished men became, still the more Zeus distrusted them; until matters came to a head at last at Sicyon. A bull was to be sacrificed to the gods and no one could decide which parts should be their portion and which part men's. Finally they called on Prometheus to be the judge. He went away alone and flayed the skin off a massive bull and made two leather bags with it. Then he jointed the carcass, separated the fat from the meat, the meat from the bone and the innards from all of them. He put the meat in one of the leather bags but hid it under the least appetising parts of the offal and the stomach. The bones, on the other hand, he put in the second bag beneath a layer of rich white fat. Then he offered both these bags to Zeus saying, 'Choose – whatever you take will be your portion for eternity.' Seeing the generous fat Zeus did not hesitate, that was the bag he took.

His roar of anger when he discovered its contents, the skull, the thigh-bones, the shoulder blades, the ribs, the whole sturdy structure on which the flesh had lived – that roar shook the heavens, set men trembling, for they did not know the thunder told only their advantage. 'Meat men may have gained by this trick. But they'll have to eat it raw,' said Zeus. And he hid all fire from them immediately. But Prometheus watched him, knew his hiding-places, and later he went to Athene, begged her to let him on to Mount Olympus by some back way, and so secretly she did.

He took a wooden torch with him, coated well with pitch. He crept up to the blazing chariot of the sun and thrust the torch between its wheel-spokes. The wood and pitch took flame immediately. Then he cut a glowing splinter from it and hid this in a huge ribbed stalk of the fennel plant, put out his torch and stole away – going faster and more openly the further from Olympus he got; in the end he might have been Hermes riding the air with wings upon his feet, brandishing his fire-stalk, shouting triumph to the wind. Back on earth he lit fires in all the halls and encampments of mankind with the splinter he took from the fennel stalk; the good smell of roasting meat would rise from their hearths till the end of time in consequence. But from then on too when they sacrificed to Zeus men laid only the bones of their beasts on his altars.

Zeus determined to revenge himself; his revenge on man is that other story of the maiden called Pandora. But Prometheus he took and had chained on a mountain-top right opposite the place where Atlas held up the sky. Then he sent an eagle to tear at his liver; each night by Zeus' command Prometheus' liver renewed itself, so that his suffering could continue day after day, year after year, century on century.

Aeons later in return for some advice the hero Hercules would free Prometheus from his torment. But that too is quite another story.

GREEK

DEATH

... death hath ten thousand several doors
For men to take their exits; and 'tis found
They go on such strange geometrical hinges,
You may open them both ways ...
> *John Webster, The Duchess of Malfi*

... I had seen birth and death
But had thought they were different; ...
> *T. S. Eliot*

In many mythologies death is seen as not necessarily part of the original scheme of things, but rather as an aberration, arrived at accidentally or as the result of some man's folly or wickedness. Thus Adam and Eve were disobedient, Pandora inquisitive, the men in the African chameleon story impatient, the woman in the Chinese story lazy, others were stupid or greedy or forgetful. Most of the transgressions seem minor, though, hardly worthy of such enormous punishment. The trickery and theft involved in the acquisition of fire did deserve death more, perhaps – yet what would life have been without fire? So how was its theft to be avoided? And so, how death? Thus in a way these fire/death myths, where death is the price of such a fundamental means of life, make a bridge between this first mythical view of death as an aberration, and the other more philosophical view where it is considered a natural and inevitable part of the patterning of creation.

This latter view is implicit, I think, even in the curious story of Adapa, the Babylonian Adam, who though he rouses the god's ire in the first place by exceeding what were thought to be his powers, nevertheless behaves in a perfectly proper manner thereafter and so is quite forgiven. In his case, unlike those stories where death is due to failure to obey, he brings it upon mankind precisely because he does obey. It would seem intolerable if the story did not leave one too with a sense of inevitability, as if even the gods could not help themselves.

Other myths are much more straightforward. The Hindu one indeed is quite practical and logical – faced with the results of over-population the Brahma reluctantly summons death to balance it (even though Death herself takes much convincing that her task is a proper one). Again, and more metaphysically, in an American Indian story quoted elsewhere, a man who asks to live for ever gets turned to stone. And similarly, in this collection there is a very simple yet particularly wise and beautiful story from Africa in which men and tortoises accept death as the price of their having children, and only stone does not want them and so need never die. It is a less hectic and certainly more democratic inversion of the Hindu story perhaps. In some ways too, coming to terms as it does with death in this life, here and now, it seems a maturer view than the more familiar Biblical one that regrets an Eden in which we were both childless and without knowledge;

*and which in its Christian sequel, accepts death mainly because a
paradise is promised thereafter. It offers an actual resurrection of the
living, that is, against a possible resurrection of the dead.*

Pandora

¶ When he heard of Prometheus' success, Zeus was beside himself
with rage. The humiliation he had suffered hung and festered in his
mind. Seldom had the Gods seen their king so angry. For days he
thundered and they dared not approach him. He became quieter,
but still he brooded and slowly his rage formed into a plan of
revenge. The punishment of the criminal he could deal with –
indeed already had. It was man – man who had conspired in cheat-
ing and defying him – who must be made to pay for accepting the
gift. And then slowly a smile of quite unmatched cunning crossed
the face of the King of the Gods. Such a gift must be matched – no,
surpassed. As the thought crystallized in his mind the God laughed
aloud at his own duplicity. A gift indeed. One they would never
forget, and be quite unable to resist despite the warnings of their
friend the Titan. Let it not be said that the King of the Gods was
niggardly to the race of men. And again he laughed.

Hearing his laugh the gods were relieved. They returned to his
presence to hear his bidding. Addressing them he told them of his
plan: to give to man a solace and a helpmeet to comfort him and
attend him in his every need. 'We have perhaps been hard in dealing
with this race. But now we shall befriend them with a gift that far
surpasses that of the charlatan Prometheus. A gift to warm his
heart and home. We shall give him woman. Fair, seductive, mild.
Yet full of gentle craft and guile; skilled in all the arts of hearth and
home, and in the gentler arts that mould men to their will.'

So saying, Zeus set each to an allotted task. 'Haephaestos, you
shall take the earth and mixing it with water, mould from it the
body of a lovely girl. Give her a voice as sweet as honey and human
power to move. The face as fair as an immortal goddess, her form

lithe and supple to enchant and lead men from their cares.' Athene was to teach the girl to weave and clothe her in shining garments. Aphrodite, Goddess of Love, poured all manner of charms upon her head, and Hermes, Messenger to Zeus, endowed her with grace and winning ways. When she was formed, the Graces gave her golden necklaces, and for her head the Seasons wove spring flowers into a crown. Athene clothed her in a robe of silver caught with a belt of gold and covered her head with a fine-spun veil delicately embroidered.

When all was done, they took her to Zeus who praised their skill and felt himself drawn to the enchanting creature. But hardening his heart he summoned Hermes and directed him to take her down to earth. 'Take her where the man Epimetheus, brother to that meddlesome wretch Prometheus, cannot fail to see her on his return from the fields. Returning once more alone to a night of solitude, how shall he not, foolish man, be blinded by her charms and take her home with him.' The God's laugh rang round the heavens and echoed down on earth. 'And we shall call her Pandora. For name she must have, and she is our gift to man and bearer of our other gifts to him.' Hermes took her by the hand and led her down.

Epimetheus was a different man entirely from his brother. Slower and less full of craft; a farmer and a simple man. Returning home that evening he paused to linger by the cool waters of a stream. Gazing into its clear depths, he became aware of a reflection other than his own rippling and sparkling in its depths. Turning round he was struck full in the eyes by the radiance of the setting sun. Dazzled and momentarily blinded, he yet thought he glimpsed some figure standing in the sun's light. He blinked, but when his sight had cleared, the vision was still there. It was no illusion, but the loveliest creature he had ever seen. Familiar and yet like nothing he had ever known. He stood and stared. She spoke:

'You must be Epimetheus. They told me I would find you here.'

'Who are they? And who are you?' he stammered in confusion.

'They call me Pandora, and I am their gift to you.'

'What gift and whose?' he asked again, with something stirring in his mind at what he could not understand, not quite remember.

'The immortal Gods on high Olympus, seeing the hard life you live below, have of their kindness to men sent me down to you. I am to be your companion and your aid; to bring you all those gentle gifts you do not know, and be your comfort and your help.'

She looked up then and smiled. Epimetheus was enchanted and allowed his half-formed doubts to sink back in his mind. What if his brother had once warned him against accepting gifts from Gods. Surely even he could not have found it in his heart to refuse such beauty. Could such a form contain evil? No, this could not be what he meant. And, taking her by the hand, accepting the gift of Zeus, Epimetheus led her to his home and made the woman Pandora his wife.

As the days went by Epimetheus continued to marvel at his luck. His life was changed. No longer did the labour of the day seem pointless; the hours endless. His thoughts were filled with her who would be waiting for his return at the end of each day, she with whom to share the pleasures of the day, enjoy the quiet hours of evening. He opened both his heart and home, offering all that was his to give. He took her into the great storeroom at the back of the house carved out of the rock. It was cool and shady there, and in it were stored all the treasures of the earth culled by Epimetheus over the seasons. He spread out his hands in pride, displaying the richness.

'All this is yours, Pandora, to use as you please. Everything I have is yours.'

He took her round showing the tall ranged jars of wine and oil. Sticky jars of honey round which the bees droned. Earthen crocks of grain to be ground for bread. Bunches of dark grapes and musky smelling apricots with the summer's fragrance still in them. Wrinkling apples, figs, left to dry. Hard cheeses smelling of the goats. Purple olives, skeins of pungent onions and garlic hung from the roof. All this and more – fruits of a year's struggle with the earth, and proof against the harshness of a long winter when the earth was less generous.

She wandered behind him in the gloomy cavern. It was cool and refreshing after the sticky summer heat of the house. Touching, smelling, breathing deep of the ripe musty smell, she enjoyed the wealth her husband offered. In the furthest corner, scarcely visible at first, but bigger and darker than the rest, she came upon a curious jar. A writhing contorted pattern of disturbing shapes covered its surface. Her curiosity was aroused.

'And what is in this fine jar, my husband?' she asked him.

Epimetheus turned round. For a moment his eyes dwelt on the lovely figure of his wife. Then he saw the jar on which her hand rested. Quickly he came over, attempting to draw her away. She shook him off impatiently.

'Why, what is this secret?' she laughed coyly up at him. 'What is this you will not share. Surely you will not deny me so soon after your fine promises?'

'No, no, no,' Epimetheus stammered. He was embarrassed by her taunts however charmingly spoken. And it was true, it was hard to deny her. 'I had forgotten. I had not thought you would notice the jar. It has been hidden and forgotten these many years. Better not touch it; leave it be. It is no concern of ours, indeed, it is not mine at all.' Again he tried to draw her gently away. But she was not to be so easily distracted. Her curiosity, that gift or curse which the Gods had given her, was now at a fever pitch. She could not control the excitement in her voice. She wheedled and cajoled but he would tell her nothing more than that the jar had been there for as long as he could remember. His brother he said knew more about it than he, and had always warned him neither to touch nor open it.

'It seems that it could bring great evil on mankind. It is one of the mysteries and better not to question the wisdom of the Gods.'

At this she laughed aloud in mockery. 'Ah, your brother the great Prometheus! We all know what happened to him! Shame on you to be so under his thumb.'

Epimetheus' ruddy face flushed a dark red. He opened his mouth to speak, but he could not find the words. His expression was mixed anger and sorrow. Before he spoke she had seen her mistake. She lightly laughed off her own irritation.

'Well, what does it matter after all. You are right. What is one jar amongst so many.' And taking his arm she walked with him from the storeroom, casting a lingering glance behind her at the mysterious jar. 'It is not right that we should allow your brother's words to come between us, nor the jar itself. Forget my words, my dear, for indeed I shall.' Epimetheus sighed and smiled down at her in relief. The matter was never mentioned between them again.

But Pandora did not forget the jar. During the long days she spent alone in the house, and particularly whilst sitting at her loom weaving the fine cloth as Athene had taught her, she found her thoughts returning again and again to the jar. Her mind seethed with questions; her curiosity so consumed her that there was soon little space in her thinking for anything else. At times she would leap up from where she sat to run to the storeroom to see whether the jar was still there: to touch it as though in some way she could divine its secret. Once she put her ear to its rough exterior and thought she heard, or rather felt, a low buzzing or humming from within. More than once she found herself standing by the jar not knowing quite how she came to be there. It was as though some force outside her, over which she had no control, had drawn her irresistibly to the spot. She was half frightened, half excited to find her hand trembling at the lip of the jar.

Finally the day came when she could contain her curiosity no longer. All that summer the heat had been intense. Every day was hotter than the last till it seemed that the earth itself would burst into flames. She lay on her couch at midday, oppressed by the heat and the restless droning of insects. They were bigger, blacker, fatter than she remembered. She could bear it no longer. Rising from the couch, she made her way as in a trance to the cool recesses of the store-chamber. She was quite calm as she moved inevitably towards her destination.

The jar stood where it had always been – waiting. It seemed to throb and the humming though still low, was quite distinct. Her fingers slid over the tight skin which covered its mouth; her long fingernails picked at the wax which held it firm. She was caught between shame and curiosity, but felt no guilt at what she was about to do. Almost of their own accord her fingers continued their work. Faster and more persistently they attacked the wax.

There was a sharp crack. The last long curling rind of wax dropped to the ground. The seal was broken. She paused; waited. Then, setting both hands to the jar, she pulled away the skin which still concealed its contents. The jar stood open. It did not seem such a terrible thing.

There was a rustling as though some creature long asleep was stirring in its lair. She backed away, fear mounting in her as she watched the jar. The muted throbbing increased in volume until it had become an angry whine; its fierce pitch stung her ears and she covered them with her hands to cut it out. But she could not cover her eyes, and as Pandora watched mesmerized, something began to emerge from the open mouth of the jar. Black hands clutched at the rim, seething dark shapes fought and struggled to escape. The first shape burst free and flopped on to the floor, blinking its huge blind eyes against the light, stretching creaking wings and feelers long cramped and dry. It was followed thick and fast by others and yet more of the creatures. All were like the first, loathsome rustling shades, the colours of night, jostling, buzzing, flapping. It seemed as though the swarming would never end. Pandora could neither move nor cry out. She cowered sickened where she was, helplessly watching.

Now they were beginning to dart and blunder about the chamber, their bodies brushing against the rocky walls. Their great wings creaked and groaned as they cast around desperately in search of . . . Pandora knew it was herself they sought. The air was darkened with their presence, thick with their stench and the ever mounting noise of their droning cry. The jar stood empty and silent. Pandora reached out a hand to cover it in a feeble hope to prevent further horrors. As she moved they saw her. With a shriek as of lost souls they descended on her. They stung and stung and stung again. All the pains of the world entered Pandora at that moment – pains more terrible than the world had ever known. Now she cried out, but her shrieks were smothered by the fierce cacophony of their sound. She sank to the ground, overwhelmed by their malevolence.

Then they were gone. Gone in search of their next victim – and the next and the next unendingly, until all men were visited with the suffering that was Zeus' revenge. Pandora, giver of all things and herself the gift of the gods to men, was the first to feel the pain of that other gift. She who in releasing the evils long pent up in the jar, first brought suffering on mankind. Sickness, pain, strife, war, falsehood, famine, oppression, slavery, madness, old age, loss and grief – all those evils which let death into the world. As she lay sobbing with the pain, she understood what it was she had done: how fate had used and driven her.

Returning from his day in the fields, Epimetheus heard Pandora's cries. Troubled and apprehensive, he ran to find her, calling her name as he went. On the threshold he was met by the same ravening swarm. They descended on their second victim, who sank beneath the onslaught of their attack. Then once again they were off; off into the world to spread their gift.

With the pain still coursing through his body, Epimetheus went in search of the woman. He found her struggling to cover the mouth of the jar with her body. A small shape like those which had gone before was fighting to get past her. Epimetheus pushed her roughly to one side and thrust the feeble creature back into the jar. It flopped to the bottom with a moan of despair. Epimetheus slapped on the cover, binding it tight on to the jar, and saving forever man's only defence against despair – Hope.

Only then did he turn to where Pandora stood in shame and pain. Suffering as they were, Epimetheus could not find it in his heart to blame her. Too late he realized that she, quite as much as he, was the dupe of Zeus. Both were victims. Their only hope lay in facing together the pain and evil of the world. Without speaking they looked at each other, then turning to support one another, walked together from the chamber into a world changed forever by the cruel gift of Zeus.

GREEK

In the olden days all men would die, but their souls only went away from their bodies for five days, after that they would return, and their bodies would rise and walk again.

One man, however, had a very bad-tempered wife. She would nag him if he was late home in the evening, she would nag him if he was slow to get up in the morning, she would nag him if the corn he brought in from the field was not plump enough for her liking.

One day this man died. And perhaps because it was such a rest for him to be away from his wife's tongue the soul returned to the body after six days instead of the usual five. How the wife complained then; how much she had suffered she said, other men's souls stayed away only five days, but just look at him, he had to stay away six, how could she hold up her head again among the other women, all their husbands' souls behaved in the usual way; had he never thought how worried she might be, how lonely? She was so angry she picked up a stick and started to beat the soul before it was properly settled in the man's body. Perhaps it had simply had enough for one day; perhaps the thought of the wife's tongue for ever and ever and ever was just too much for it. Anyway the moment the woman's back was turned the soul slipped away again out of the man's body and left it lifeless on the floor. The woman waited and waited but it never returned. Since then no soul has ever returned, once a man dies his life is quite ended.

SOUTH AMERICA, PERU

¶ Once upon a time men did not die. Instead they would change their skins like snakes and return to live as new people. But then this happened. The time had come for an old woman, mother of a large family, to change her skin. So she called her son and daughter-in-law to heat the water for her bath. But the daughter-in-law was a particularly lazy woman, she did not build the fire and set the water to heat upon it, instead she fetched water from outside that the rays of the sun had warmed and filled her mother-in-law's bath with that. Nor did she think to confess what she had done, thus the old woman climbed into the bath regardless and lay down expecting all to be as usual. But at once she cried out very loudly, bringing everyone running to her, to find that rather than the old skin peeling away from her body leaving her renewed and beautiful, all her bones and flesh and joints had disintegrated and were not to be put back together again. Thus the old woman never rose from her bath, never took up the life that was hers and due to her.

The daughter-in-law hid her guilt from everyone. But one night the mother returned to see her in a dream. The woman heard her speak. 'Because you have done this to me,' the spirit said, 'because I have died as a result of your idleness, so must everyone know what it is to suffer death. Death is no longer to be avoided.'

And so it was. And so it is all men must die.

CHINESE

¶ Unkulunkulu had created the earth and placed man on it to enjoy its fruits. But he had not told man what would become of him; the people kept on asking and asking themselves but finding no answer to the question they determined at last to send a messenger to Unkulunkulu himself. The chameleon was the messenger they chose, and when he reached heaven and explained his errand Unkulunkulu said, 'Tell my people man shall not die.' The chameleon set out for home again. But the journey was pleasant. He kept on stopping to eat and sleep. The people grew impatient, they began to think that he would never come so they sent another messenger to the God, the lizard this time, who ran very fast and said to Unkulunkulu, 'The people want to know what will become of them.' But Unkulunkulu grew angry, not liking to be asked the same question twice. He said, 'Tell the people they must all die.' The lizard ran home again very fast, passing the chameleon who was not far away from the people's village now, but had stopped yet again to taste mulberries. 'What will become of us, what will become of us?' they asked the lizard as soon as they saw him. 'Unkulunkulu said to tell you that you must all die,' the lizard said. The people fell to weeping and wailing, they were weeping so loudly that when the chameleon came wandering in not very long afterwards looking well-fed and pleased with himself and said, 'Great Unkulunkulu says you shall not die,' no one heard except for one man and he did not believe him. So that was the end of it, people knew what would happen to them, that they would all die, and so they have always died ever since.

AFRICA

¶ The Heaven Shining Great August Spirit told his grandson, his Augustness Heaven Plenty Earth Plenty Heaven's Sun Height Prince Ruddy Rice Ear Plenty, 'You must descend from heaven. In future your life will be on earth.'

'As you command me, so I do,' the young man said. He left his heavenly seat, divided the clouds and made himself a road through them, then floated over the floating bridge of heaven and down to the peak of the southern mountain. There he met a beautiful girl and asked her whose daughter she was.

'My father is The Spirit That Owns The Great Mountain. And I am Princess Blossoming Brilliantly As The Trees.'

'Have you brothers? Have you sisters?'

'I have an older sister. Her name is Princess As Long As The Rocks.'

Prince Ruddy Rice Ear Plenty said, 'You'd better know that my one and only wish just now is to sleep with you all night.'

'It is not for me to decide. You must ask my father, The Spirit That Owns The Great Mountain.'

The Spirit That Owns The Great Mountain said, 'I shall be honoured if you marry my daughter, Princess Blossoming As Brilliantly As The Trees. On the other hand you must also take to wife her older sister, my other daughter, the Princess As Long As The Rocks.'

But when Princess As Long As The Rocks came to Prince Ruddy Rice Ear Plenty he found her as ugly as he had found her younger sister beautiful. So he turned his eyes away from her and sent her out of his presence and he spent his wedding night with Princess Blossoming Brilliantly As The Trees, alone.

Princess As Long As The Rocks went back to her father. In the morning The Spirit That Owns The Great Mountain sent a message to Prince Ruddy Rice Ear Plenty. 'Now I am ashamed to speak to you,' he said, 'for I gave you both my daughters to marry with good reason. Through my younger daughter the Princess Blossoming As Brilliantly As The Trees, your August Offspring would have blossomed as brilliantly as the flowers on the trees. And through my elder daughter the Princess As Long As The Rocks, let the wind blow and the rain fall they would not have been swept away; indeed they would have lived for as long as the rocks themselves. Now, however, because you have refused my elder daughter, though the blossoming of your August Offspring may still be brilliant it will also be as brief as that of the flowers on the trees.'

And that is why the lives of their Augustnesses, our August Heavenly Sovereigns are never never long.

JAPANESE

¶ Adapa was a man but among men the wisest, created by Ea to rule in the city of Eridu. He served the god in his temple and in his own house. He baked bread and fetched fresh water and each day alone he set the god's table. He was also a fisherman. When the city larders were empty he went to the harbour, untied his boat and set out into the waves of the broad bright sea, while the wind blew strongly and filled his sails. And when he came to the place where he knew he would find fish he would lower them and cast out his nets. One day as he began to fish the sea was smooth as glass. But the South Wind swelled all at once, breathed mightily, capsized his boat and blew him to the bottom of the sea among the fishes. Adapa was angry. He cursed the South Wind and broke its wings into many pieces. For seven days then it did not blow at all. In the sky the great god Anu asked:

'Why has the South Wind not blown for seven days?' And one answered him:

'Because the man Adapa cursed it, and broke its wings into many pieces.'

Anu was angry. He shouted, 'Bring the man here,' and began to prepare a death for him. But Adapa was Ea's son, so Ea sent for Adapa first and warned him what to do in heaven.

'You must wear mourning clothes,' he said. 'You must not cut your hair. When you reach the heavenly gate you will find two gods waiting and they will ask "Why are you in mourning, Adapa?" And you will say to them, "I am in mourning for Tammuz and Gazzida," and they will smile for they will be none other than

Tammuz and Gazzida and they will take you to Anu and plead your cause with him. You will be offered bread but you must not eat, for it will be the bread of death. You will be offered water and you must not drink, for it will be the water of death. But when they fetch you a garment you may put that on; when they bring you oil you may anoint yourself.'

And so it was. Adapa put on mourning clothes, rent them and let his hair hang loose. And when the messenger from Anu came for him he followed, weeping, on the road to heaven. The two gods were waiting at the East Gate just as Ea had promised him. They asked,

'Why do you look like that, Adapa, for whom are you mourning?'

'I am mourning for Tammuz and Gazzida because they have left my land for ever.' Tammuz and Gazzida looked at each other and smiled. They led Adapa into the hall of Anu, God of heaven.

Anu asked him, 'Why did you act the god and break the wings of the South Wind so that for seven days he could not blow?'

Adapa said, 'I was catching fish on a sea as smooth as glass, doing harm to no one when the wind blew suddenly and sent me down among the fishes. And so I was angry and cursed him with all my heart.'

'That was an arrogance,' said Anu. 'That a mere man should act as god.' But Tammuz and Gazzida standing beside Adapa spoke calmly and soothed the anger of great Anu. At last he said to them, 'It was Ea's fault in the beginning, giving him such mighty powers. Now since he has them it is too late to mend, I will see him eat the Bread of Life. Fetch it. Fetch the Water also. Adapa and his kin shall live for ever.'

But Adapa remembered what Ea had told him. When the bread was offered, expecting the Bread of Death he would not eat; and when the water, expecting the Water of Death he would not drink. But he put on the garment that they offered him, he anointed himself with the oil that they had brought.

Anu spoke in amazement to Adapa. 'So, it is done,' he said. 'I offered eternal life and you refused it. And now in the fullness of years you shall die and your children also and your children's children.'

Adapa said, 'I did what my lord has commanded me to do.'

Anu said, 'Thus in the meridian of heaven my will prevails. It is not for a man to break the wings of the wind.' Then Adapa left Anu's heavenly palace and returned to his home in Eridu. There he went on baking bread and fetching pure water, setting the table for the god, and fishing for his people when their larders were empty. But in the fullness of his years he grew old and died. So we have all done since, his children and his children's children.

Let us curse Adapa then who brought death on us. Let him not feel the peace of heaven, let him not know our quieter dreams, or any of the contentments that fill the lives of men. For the rest of us, let our sufferings ease, let our diseases lighten, let us be at peace.

BABYLONIAN

¶ There were four worlds before our own. The first and second were too small and the third was inundated by a great flood when the water monster Ticholtsodi came looking for his children – they were so beautiful Coyote had stolen them and hidden them in his bundle. But although the fourth world was a much bigger and better one, the men and the women quarrelled there among themselves; and after a while, Coyote still hiding the water monster's children, the flood rose again and, as they had before in the third world the people piled together the mountains of the four directions, and planted a reed on top which grew and grew until it had reached the sky. And then the people climbed the reed, hoping to find themselves a fifth world at the top of it.

Badger went first. He dug his way up and through the sky, but instead of emerging on to dry land found himself in the middle of a muddy lake. He shouted down to the rest of the people, and they did not know what to do next, the flood waters rising higher and higher behind them. They feared themselves drowned in any event. At last Locust said, 'Let me see what I can do about it,' and up he flew into the fifth world and met there swimming on the surface of the muddy lake four swans, the colours of the four earth corners, black, blue, yellow and white. 'Where have you come from?' they asked Locust. When Locust had told them his story and begged them to let his people join them in the fifth world the swans said, 'Certainly they may. Provided only that they can do what we can, each one of them, that is pass an arrow through their bodies from top to bottom.' For swans are made differently from other creatures and this is something they were able to do. Locust said, 'My people will do as you ask. Only, in return, each of you must do as I do now and pass an arrow from one side of your body to the other.' For Locust too was a different shape from others, his spine particularly narrow. At which the swans agreed to let Locust's people enter their world without any conditions at all. And this they did, carrying all their possessions in bundles on their backs. Because Coyote's bundle, however, still contained the two children of the water monster, the monster Ticholtsodi also followed them, bringing the flood waters with him. But this time the people saw the monster's horns sticking up from the middle of the lake, and at last they began to guess the reason for the floods. Each in turn opened his bundle and showed its contents, and when it came to Coyote's turn the two children were revealed. The people took them back to the water monster, immediately he went away taking the flood waters with him, and left the people standing on an island in the middle of the swamp.

But the island was still much too small for the people to live on. Because of the swamp they could not move forward or back, to the right or to the left. So they prayed with one voice to the god of the darkness who came immediately and cut open the cliffs that surrounded the swamp, thus little by little the waters drained away. But finding the earth around them still too soft for them to walk upon they prayed again, to the four winds this time, which rose and blew for four days on end until the earth dried out and they were able to walk where the swamp had been. They piled up the mud then to make a mountain at each of the four corners, which kept on growing as the earth kept expanding. And when the earth had reached almost its furthest point they took the sun and moon and flung them into the sky. The sun was very near the earth still but as the earth kept on expanding outwards so the sun and the moon kept on moving away from it. Until the fifth day when all at once the sun stopped dead and stood there over the people's heads burning and burning.

The people did not know what to do. The sun burned and burned, it burned the leaves off the grass, it burned the hair off their heads, it dried up all the lakes and rivers. They said, 'What will become of us, what kind of life will we be able to lead if we can't persuade the sun to go further away from us?' They prayed and prayed but still nothing happened, still the sun went on burning and burning. At last the chief's wife said, 'I will offer myself. Let us see what happens.' And she went and lay down by herself under the sun's eye. Gradually, in the heat of it, her body grew cold, her life's breath slipped from her mouth and departed; soon she had disappeared from men's sight altogether and they wept because this was the first death there had ever been among them. But immediately they noticed that the sun had begun to move again. 'So that is the sun's price,' they said. 'One of us has to die each day.' And they were afraid, until a wise man went to the place of emergence and looked back into the fourth world and saw the chief's wife sitting there combing her hair. So the people knew that the rest of them would join her when they died and stopped being frightened after all.

One night not long after this the moon halted in the very middle of the sky. But when the wise man who had been to the place of emergence fell sick and died, the moon too began to move again.

Coyote had guessed the way of this world now, the price of their life on it. 'Each day,' he said, 'one of us must die, each night one of our tribe or another must die also. Only then will the sun continue to move for us by day and the moon to travel all the night.'

NORTH AMERICA *Navaho*

¶ The Grandfather Brahma in the beginning created living beings. So great his fiery energy – so many the beings he created – they multiplied and multiplied until there was no place for them to breathe, no place for them to live. The earth groaned with the weight and was ready to sink into the sea from which it came. At last the Brahma's energy turned to anger. He sent out mighty tongues of fire, he burned heaven and earth and air and all the creatures that moved or that stayed still.

Rudra the pillar said, 'Pity them grandfather. You made them, why do you burn them everywhere?' And the Brahma replied, 'There is no space for them to breathe, there is no space for them to live. The earth groans, soon their weight will cause it to sink back into the sea again. I have thought, I have thought; yet as I can see no way of checking their increase, I have grown angry. So I breathe out fire and burn them.' The pillar Rudra then said, 'Oh Lord of the Universe, of the thirty-three gods, do not be angry. Have mercy on them all, on all the community of living creatures, moving and still, on all the lakes and ponds and all the trees and grasses. Find some other way of controlling their increase; let them live within the cycle of birth and death, so that they may come and they may go, and you need not destroy them with your blasts of fiery anger.'

Brahma heard him and Brahma pondered. He drew back the fire and hid it again within his body. And there emerged instead from his every aperture, ears, eyes, nose and mouth and anus, a woman, dark-eyed, dark-faced and clothed in red garments. She had red rims to her eyes, red palms to her hands, red soles to her feet. She stood at Brahma's right hand and he said to her, 'Your name is Death. You must go forth and destroy all creatures without exception and that way you will win favour in my eyes.'

But the goddess Death wept to hear the task she had been given. She said, 'Great Spirit spare me. The task I must perform will unbalance the order of things and I will be made unclean. How can I destroy old men and children, how can I harm those who have done me none? Their families will hate me for ever, their tears will never let me forget it is I that have destroyed them. Have mercy on me. Grant me this favour instead. Let me depart and practise asceticism, for that is a task that belongs to the order of things.'

God said, 'I made you, Death, that you might destroy. Go and destroy therefore without delay. It must be. You have no choice. Go and do as I command.'

But Death went on standing before him with her head bowed and said nothing more. Again and again the Brahma spoke to her and still she remained silent. At last God looked down upon his people and all his anger died. And Death slipped away from him without any promise to obey. She went to Dhenake, the place of pilgrimage, and she practised that hardest of all asceticisms, standing on one foot for fifteen thousand million years. When the Brahma said to her again, 'Death, you must obey me and destroy,' she ignored him, stood on the other foot for twenty thousand million years, and then for ten million years she lived with the wild beasts. For another twenty thousand years she ate nothing but air and for eight thousand years she stood silently in water. Finally on a peak of the Himalayas she stood on one toe for a thousand million years and at last the Brahma was satisfied.

He said to her gently, 'Daughter, why don't you do as I tell you?'

'Have mercy, Grandfather,' she said.

The Brahma said, 'Death, you are worthy and you are virtuous. You will not destroy order, rather you will restore it. For now there is no space for men to breathe or live, the earth is sinking beneath their weight. Men and women will not hate you, the gods will honour you and watch over you. You will be a man among men, a woman among women, a eunuch among eunuchs.'

But still Death, weeping, put her hands together and said to the Brahma, 'No.'

'It must be. It is already, righteous one. Each one of these tears that fall from your eyes is a disease that will soon afflict mankind. You will come to each man at the appointed time and you will be righteous still, you will be virtuous. You will employ desire and anger together to end the life of creatures. Welcome them then, desire and anger. Join with them and destroy; destroy.'

Death still did not want to be called Death, but now also she feared that the Brahma would curse her forever. So she began her life's work, taking breath from the creatures that the Brahma had made when their time had come, setting them to face their end between desire and anger. And the tears she let fall became the diseases that beset them.

So the Brahma made death to destroy men at the proper time, so that they would have space to live and breathe on earth, so that the earth would not sink beneath the waters.

INDIA *Hindi*

Tortoises, Men and Stones

¶ God created the tortoise, men, and stones. Of each he created male and female. He gave life to tortoises and men, but not to the stones. None could have children, and when they became old they did not die but became young again.

The tortoise, however, wished to have children, and he went to God. But God said:

'I have given you life, but I have not given you permission to have children.'

But the tortoise came to God again to make his request, and finally God said:

'You always come and ask for children. Do you realize that when the living have had several children they must die?'

But the tortoise said:

'Let me see my children and then die.' Then God granted his wish.

When man saw that the tortoise had children, he too wanted children. God warned man, as he had the tortoise, that he must die. But man also said:

'Let me see my children and then die.'

That is how death and children came into the world. Only the stones did not want to have children, and so they never die.

AFRICA, NIGERIA *Nupe*

FOOD PLANTS

Except a corn of wheat fall into
the ground, and die, it abideth alone:
But if it die, it bringeth forth much fruit. . . .
St. John's Gospel

Now I am terrified at the Earth, it is that calm and
patient,
It grows such sweet things out of such corrup-
tions . . . .
Walt Whitman

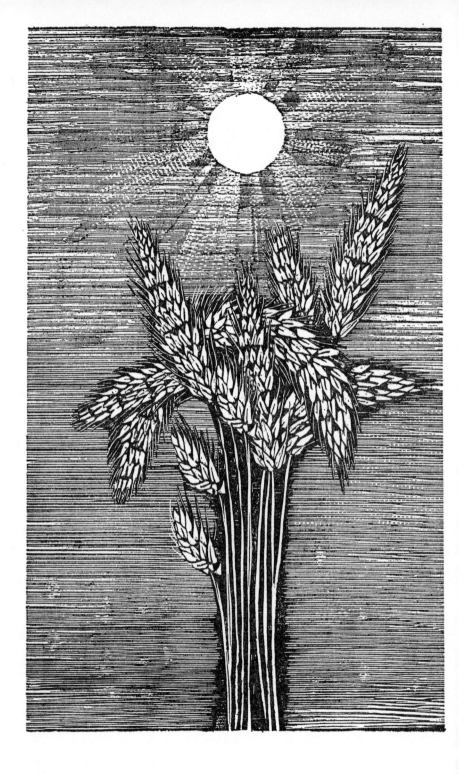

Here, in this section, unlike the others I have chosen to concentrate on one type of story only, first because it is a good deal more interesting than all the other types which mainly involve the god or gods giving their creation a lesson in elementary agriculture, and second and more importantly, because through all its forms it is not only universal but also wholly fundamental. Indeed since it states more explicitly than any what has come to be the theme of this whole book, it is where I first began to see its pattern, more or less.

For it is the reverse of the story where life has to be paid for by death. Here instead is the slain god or human (or animal – in the oddest of the versions here, even a swarm of bees) from whose body or bodies, flesh and blood, springs the food of life which, translated literally, means the staple food plant of the area from which any story comes; rice in Asia, yam and taro in the Pacific, maize in Central and Northern America, and so on. Taken more figuratively it develops via the more sophisticated myth cycles, first into a less particular vegetation myth of a god whose yearly death and rebirth is both the image of and also the cause of the growth of plants and crops in general – Adonis in the Greek myth for instance, Osiris in the Egyptian myth included here; and from thence into the Christian myth itself, of the death and resurrection of Christ. Where apart from the Cross being described so frequently as the tree, it has shed all vegetable connections and simply sees men as themselves reborn, redeemed directly by the body and blood of the slain and then risen God.

It is the most profound and inevitable of myths seen from one direction; that is in reconciliation with the fact of and necessity for death. Thus St. John . . . 'Except a corn of wheat fall into the ground, and die. . .' Seen from the other, not in the acceptance of the death that has occurred or must occur but in its preordaining, whether of the child chosen to die so that his blood may feed the harvest, or of the Christ figure doomed by God to be crucified before he was even conceived, it can seem the most uncompromising, even the most primitive myth of all. Certainly it is one of the most dangerous. It has been the justification for human sacrifice the world over; this in turn ranging from the death of a single willing victim to the massive and hysterical sacrifice of thousands as in the Aztec rituals, where it was feared that without such mighty meals of human hearts and blood the sun, the source of life – and harvest – would never rise again. Which demonstrates precisely the danger of taking myth too seriously, as the literal truth, instead of as an image of the truth.

More frivolously – but still it's intriguing ; the British almost alone see their ritually slain figure – John Barleycorn – as the source not of bread, that is of solid food, but beer.

¶ 'I was sown in the morning twilight, reaped in the evening twilight, thrown into the granary in order to be brewed into small beer at Easter and baked into pastries at Christmas.'

FINLAND *Mordvin*

¶ In a big lake said to be connected with the sea, lived the Lord Scorpion Fish, son of the crocodile. But his children were men who lived on earth and produced children of their own and there was not food enough for them on earth, so they came to the Lord Scorpion Fish and said, 'Lord, Lord, our father and our grandfather, we are hungry and our children are dying, tell us what we should do to save ourselves or we shall all die.' The Lord Scorpion Fish loved them and he could not bear to see them suffering. 'Kill me,' he said, 'then bury my body in the earth and you shall see what you shall see.' His children and his grandchildren wept because they loved him too, nonetheless they did what he had asked, they killed him and buried him deep in the rich earth beside the lake. And in a little while plants grew; gourds from his head and maize from his bones and rice from his flesh. The children and grandchildren of the Lord Scorpion Fish gathered the gourds and the maize and the rice and ate until they were not hungry any more and their children grew strong and did not die. So it was from that time on because of the gifts they had been given by their father and grandfather, the Lord Scorpion Fish.

INDONESIA *Amarassi*

¶ Once upon a time all men lived up in the sky with God. They were his servants. The earth below was a bare, dry place, the sun shone on it all day, and nothing grew. God had made it nonetheless and he thought something might be done with it. So did his only son, indeed he begged God to let him visit it. And at last his father said, 'Go to earth then, but come back soon and tell me if living things should be created there.' So his son departed cheerfully. But when he reached the earth he found he could not live for heat, he plunged deep inside it, hoping for coolness, but there was none, he grew hotter and hotter till he died, and did not come forth from the earth again.

Up in the sky God was waiting for his son. One day he said to his servants, 'I can wait no more, you must go down to earth and look for him.' So then a party of men followed God's son down, and they too found the earth very dry and hot. They were thirsty, they were hungry, they wept with misery and pain, nevertheless as God had ordered they went on hunting for his son. But though they looked for him everywhere they could not find him. At last they sent a messenger to God. 'If your son is here, he is nowhere to be found.' When God did not answer they sent another messenger. 'We are hungry, we are thirsty, the sun burns us up. If we stay here much longer we are bound to die.' Then God took pity on them, he drew water to him from the sky and let it fall as rain on the dry earth beneath. And men opened their mouths and drank and they were not thirsty any more. And where the rain fell on earth green plants sprang up, food plants among them, maize and barley, and men gathered them and ate. So then they were not hungry any more. They knew this was their reward for looking for God's son. But it was the only answer they ever got from God, for every time they sent a messenger to ask if they should still seek his son the messenger did not return to them. And so they go on looking for him still.

MADAGASCAR

¶ Long ago there were no farmers and nobody tilled the soil because there were no such plants as wheat and maize and barley. People lived instead by killing the wild beasts in the forest or by gathering honey from the wild bees. There were two brothers at that time. Yakish the elder one was wicked and a hunter, Velyuk the younger was a gatherer and a good man besides. Honey is good enough nourishment for me, he said. But Yakish said, nonsense, only meat is the proper food for the strong. One day, however, game was so scarce in the forest Yakish could make no kill, and he went to Velyuk and begged him for honey and Velyuk gladly gave him some. Finding it more sweet than he'd expected, Yakish became greedy, he asked his brother where the bees lived and Velyuk took him into the forest and showed him a hollow tree. I would like to watch the creatures for a while, said Yakish. So Velyuk smiled at him and went away. As soon as he was gone Yakish climbed the hollow tree and stole as much honey as he could carry. But since he left no offering for Keremet, the angry God ordered the bees to swarm round Yakish and sting him till he died; which they did. But all the bees died too, because a bee cannot lose his sting and live.

In a little while Velyuk returned. When he saw his dead brother lying there and the dead bees all round him he fell to the ground and lay weeping bitterly. He wept so long that night came and he fell asleep, and as he slept the god spoke to him in a dream; take a young calf, he said, pour water over it, mingle the dead bees with the drops that fall from its body, and dig the bees into the earth. When Velyuk woke he did just what he had been ordered, and thus became the first farmer, this plot in the forest the first arable ground, and his the first sowing. Soon grass grew up from the ground, some with ears, some with strings and some with grains like a bee-swarm in a tree. Velyuk called the first kind wheat, the second barley, the third maize, he gave some of their grains to Keremet in honour of his gift, but the rest he ground and mixed with water and ate instead of honey. And that was the first porridge, and when he baked it, that was the first bread.

As for dead Yakish; the worms that kill young bees crawled out of his heart, and the mice that steal bread were moulded from his body.

RUSSIA, SIBERIA

John Barleycorn

There was three kings into the east,
Three kings both great and high,
And they hae sworn a solemn oath
John Barleycorn should die.

They took a plough and plough'd him down,
Put clods upon his head,
And they hae sworn a solemn oath
John Barleycorn was dead.

But the cheerful Spring came kindly on,
And show'rs began to fall;
John Barleycorn got up again,
And sore surpris'd them all.

The sultry suns of summer came,
And he grew thick and strong:
His head weel arm'd wi' pointed spears,
That no one should him wrong.

The sober Autumn enter'd mild,
When he grew wan and pale;
His bending joints and drooping head
Show'd he began to fail.

His colour sicken'd more and more,
He faded into age;
And then his enemies began
To show their deadly rage.

They've taen a weapon long and sharp,
And cut him by the knee;
Then ty'd him fast upon a cart,
Like a rogue for forgerie.

They laid him down upon his back,
And cudgell'd him full sore.
They hung him up before the storm,
And turn'd him o'er and o'er.

They filled up a darksome pit
With water to the brim,
They heaved in John Barleycorn –
There, let him sink or swim!

They laid him out upon the floor,
To work him farther woe;
And still, as signs of life appear'd,
They toss'd him to and fro.

They wasted o'er a scorching flame
The marrow of his bones;
But a miller us'd him worst of all,
For he crush'd him between two stones.

And they hae taen his very heart's blood,
And drank it round and round;
And still the more and more they drank,
Their joy did more abound.

John Barleycorn was a hero bold,
Of noble enterprise;
For if you do but taste his blood,
'Twill make your courage rise.

'Twill make a man forget his woe;
'Twill heighten all his joy;
'Twill make the widow's heart to sing,
Tho' the tears were in her eye.

Then let us toast John Barleycorn,
Each man a glass in hand;
And may his great posterity
Ne'er fail in old Scotland!

Robert Burns

The Coming of the Corn

¶ In old times there dwelt on the shores of a great lake a mighty warrior. His people had all been driven far away inland by hostile tribes, but he remained behind to roam over the islands in the Lake and to send his people word of any approaching attack. His wife was dead; she had been killed by treacherous foes. He had two little boys, and he kept them with him on his wanderings by the Lake. He was a great magician as well as a man of great strength and he had no fear in his heart. The islands in the Lake were haunted by spirits or 'manitous', but the man was not afraid of them, and with his boys he paddled his canoe up and down, watching for signs of his foes. Each night he landed in a cove, and pulled his canoe far up among the trees, and slept in the woods out of the sight of travellers. But he found it very hard to get game and fish, and often his boys were very hungry.

One morning at dawn of day he rose and went to find food for breakfast. He left his little boys asleep under the trees. He walked through the forest until he came suddenly upon a wide and open red plain. There was not a tree or a rock or a blade of grass upon it. He set out across the plain, and when he reached the middle of it, he met a small man with a red feather in his cap. 'Where are you going?' said the little man. 'I am going across the plain to the woods on the other side,' said the man; 'my boys are hungry without food, and I am looking for game.' 'How strong are you?' said the little man. 'I am as strong as the human race,' said the man, 'but no stronger.' 'My name is Red Plume,' said the little man; 'we must wrestle. If you should make me fall, say to me "I have thrown you"; if you should overcome me you will never want for food, for you will have other nourishment than fish and game.' They smoked their pipes for a long while, and then they wrestled. They wrestled for a long time. The warrior was growing weak, for the little man was very strong. But at last he threw Red Plume down and cried, 'I have thrown you.' And at once the little man disappeared. When the warrior looked on the ground where his opponent had fallen, he saw only a crooked thing like an acorn, with a red tassel on it. He picked it up and looked at it, and as he looked, a voice from it said, 'Take off my outside covering; split me into many parts, and throw the parts over the plain; scatter every bit of me; throw my spine near the woods. Then in a month come back to the plain.' The warrior did as he was told, and then went back to his boys. On the way he killed a rabbit and cooked it for breakfast. He did not tell his boys what he had seen.

At the end of a month he went alone again to the plain. In the place where he had scattered the pieces of the strange object, he found blades of strange grass peeping green above the ground. And where he had thrown the pieces of the spine near the wood, little pumpkins were growing. He did not tell his boys what he had found. All summer he watched for his foes, and in the autumn he went again to the place where he had thrown down the man of the Red Plume. The plain was covered with Indian corn in the ear, and there were also pumpkins of great size near the woods. The corn was golden yellow, and red tassels grew from the top of the ears. He plucked some ears of corn and gathered some of the pumpkins and set out to find his boys. Then a voice spoke from the corn. He knew it at once to be the voice of the man of the Red Plume. It said, 'You have conquered me. If you had failed, you would still have lived, but often you would have hungered as before. Henceforth you shall never want for food, for when game and fish are scarce you will have bread. And I will never let the human race lack food if they keep me near them.' So corn came to the Indians in olden times, and never afterwards did they want for food.

When the man came to his boys, he told them what he had found. He ground some of the corn between stones, and made bread from the meal, and he cooked a pumpkin and ate it. Then he thought of his poor old father and mother far away beyond the hills, perhaps without food. So that night he took his boys and travelled far through the forest until he found his parents. He told them of his meeting with the man of the Red Plume and of the coming of the corn. And he brought them back with him to the 'manitou' islands near the shores of the great lake. And ever afterwards the fields were fruitful and corn was abundant and never failed in the land where Red Plume fell.

NORTH AMERICA, CANADA

¶ In the beginning nine families were on earth. They lived in the jungle with one of the three Virgin Dema, Satene, at a place known as the Nine Dance Grounds between Ahiolo and Varoioin.

Among them was a man called Ameta whose name meant night and he had neither wife nor children, only a dog that went hunting with him. And one day this dog put up a wild pig and chased it into a lake in which it swam until it was so exhausted it drowned in the water. Ameta dragged its body to the shore, and finding a coconut upon one of its tusks he took it home with him, wrapping it reverently in a cloth with an image of a snake's head on it. For coconuts were unknown to men before that time.

That night while he slept Satene sent a man to him in a dream. The man said, 'If the coconut is to grow, Ameta, you must plant it in the ground.' So next day Ameta planted it, and in three days it was a tall tree and in three more there was blossom on it. But when Ameta climbed the tree to gather the blossom his knife slipped and cut his own finger and the blood from his finger fell upon a leaf. After three days had passed the head of a young girl had grown from the leaf; after six days her body had appeared, and after nine a complete little girl lay ready for gathering, head and body, arms, legs, hands and feet. That night the man again appeared to Ameta. 'Wrap the maid in your snake's-head cloth,' he said, 'and take her home with you. Her name is Hainuwele and she is Satene's sister, but she will also be your daughter now.'

Hainuwele was very beautiful and like no ordinary girl. Not only did she grow to marriageable age in just three days more, but even her excrement was different from that of others', it was coral and gold and copper, it was gongs and boxes, dishes and knives. Her father gathered up all these precious things and soon he was the richest man among the nine families.

Now the time came for the great Maro Dance. That dance continued for nine nights, one night on each of the nine dance grounds. The women stood in the centre of the ground and handed out betel nuts to the men who danced in spirals round them. This year Ameta's daughter Hainuwele stood among the women. But she was no ordinary woman. The first night on the first dance ground she handed out betel nuts as the other women did. But on the second her gifts were made of coral, the men crowding the dance round her, for none wanted betel when he could have coral ornaments. On the third night she gave dishes of Chinese porcelain, on the fourth dishes again, but still more splendid ones, the fifth, bush knives, the sixth, copper boxes, the seventh, gold ear-rings, the eighth, huge and splendid gongs. The other women who still had only betel nuts to give grew increasingly envious and angry. And their men too became suspicious, they were jealous of Hainuwele's wealth. The nine families disputed it among themselves but by the ninth day they had decided to kill Hainuwele.

On the ninth night therefore they dug a pit in the middle of the ninth dancing ground, and in the course of the ninth dance all the men of one family danced closer and closer round Hainuwele, winding their spiral so tightly about her that they had soon pressed her right to the edge of the pit that they had dug and were able to cast her in, raising their voices and singing the dance song louder to drown her screams of fear. Then they threw the earth over her and having trampled it down, went on dancing over and over her until she was quite dead.

Ameta, whose name meant night, waited for Hainuwele, his daughter, to return to his hut after the dancing; he waited with his dog, his hunting companion. But Hainuwele did not return. And at last Ameta knew that his daughter had been killed. He cut nine fronds of the cocopalm and went to the ninth dancing ground and stuck them in the earth one after the other; and on the ninth frond when he took it from the earth he saw the blood and hair of Hainuwele; so he dug there; and when he had found her body, he cut it in pieces and buried it in different parts of the dance floor – all except her two arms which he saved and gave to Hainuwele's sister Satene. And all the time he cursed mankind for the murder of his daughter. But Satene meanwhile was making a gate at the centre of the dancing ground, a gate like the spiral the men danced while they were killing Hainuwele. And she ordered the nine families of men to come to her through the gate. Those who failed to tread the spiral round, she turned into deer and pigs and birds and fishes, and from that time there were animals and birds and fishes where none had been before. But those who had succeeded she struck with one of Hainuwele's arms and divided into tribes according to whether she struck them with the right arm or the left. And then, because they had murdered Hainuwele her sister, she went away and did not live any more among men in the jungle between Ahiolo and Varoioin.

Meanwhile plants had appeared on the dancing ground at the points where Ameta had buried Hainuwele, new plants that had never been known on earth, yams and taros and sweet potatoes. The two tribes of men tasted them and found them good to eat. And each year afterwards they planted again and ate them, the yam, the taro and the sweet potato; the plants that grew first from the body of Hainuwele, sister of Satene and daughter of Ameta whose name meant night; who once again had neither wife nor child in his hut, but lived there with his dog, alone.

NEW GUINEA, *West Ceram*

Isis and Osiris

¶ Long before the Pharaohs there was a great king in Egypt named Osiris, who with his wife Isis taught his people all the arts of husbandry; how to sow and reap the wheat and barley; how to grind them to flour and from the flour bake bread and honey cakes; how to plant vines and tend them, and how to tread the grapes for wine; how to cultivate fruit trees and gather and store their fruit. None of these things were known in Egypt before that time, indeed they were not known anywhere, and when he had instructed his own people Osiris travelled far beyond the land of Egypt teaching the arts he had perfected and finding new skills when they were needed, showing southerners how to irrigate the desert and terrace in-hospitable hillsides, northerners how to brew beer from barley where vines would not grow for cold.

But Osiris had a brother, Set; who lacking Osiris' power and skill and growing envious of both found forty-two like-minded men to plot the king's death with him. He took tools and made a coffin which he and his fellows carried to an assembly in the palace – it was a joke, he said, a game, everyone should try it and see how it fitted them; after all each of them was mortal and bound to die at last. So in turn men lay down in the coffin, and one would be too short, another too long for it, a third too fat to squeeze in at all, a fourth so thin it would have taken two of him. But when Osiris, smiling, offered himself there, his head met one end of the coffin, his feet reached the other, while its sides fitted his sides as flesh fits on to bone. And Set too smiled on seeing it and made a sign to his followers. They slapped the lid down upon Osiris, soldered it with molten lead and nailed it with brass nails. Then they lifted the coffin upon their shoulders, bore it out of the palace and flung it in the river Nile. So first the river took the coffin with its brass nails, then the sea tossed it hither and thither, until it was brought to shore at last on the coast of Syria. And there a tree grew up all round it, a tamerisk, its wood hiding the coffin as completely as the coffin had enclosed the body of Osiris. It happened that the King of Syria came past one day; admiring the mighty tree he ordered it to be cut down and made into one of the pillars of his house. And so it was and no one knew, not the king himself, that Osiris stood guard upon his household, winter and summer, night and day.

In Egypt meanwhile they lamented Osiris. Isis, his wife, wept most bitterly of all, she sheared off locks of her hair to show her grief, she put on a simple mourning robe and set off into the world to look for Osiris' body. For many years she wandered but heard no news of him; for so many years she found it hard at times to recall his face or to believe that he had loved her once; it would have been easier to forget that he had lived at all. But she did not forget. Day in, day out, she longed for him and grieved for him. And at last she came to Syria and hearing of the tamarisk tree in the Syrian king's house she divined at once what lay at its heart, and so offered herself as wet nurse for the King's youngest son and was taken in. No one was to know that she fed the child from her finger and not her breast; no one guessed that at night she bathed him in fire to make him immortal. She would change herself into a swallow meanwhile and swoop about the pillar mourning her lost love – Osiris, my dear one, our bed is lonely, our garden does not grow, she sang. The baby behind her kicked his feet among the flames and smiled.

This continued for many nights; until the Syrian queen came

into the chamber once and seeing her baby wrapped in fire screamed and snatched him away from it. So his immortality was lost, though not a mark of fire was found upon him. But while the people were marvelling at that, Isis revealed herself at last, and begged to have the tree cut open for her; which was done immediately and they found the coffin, upright, at the heart of the tamarisk. She opened it when they left her alone to mourn, afraid at first in case she would not recognise him now – yet then, at the sight of her husband's face her cry of grief was such that the king's eldest child hearing it died at once. All night she mourned beside Osiris, calling his name and holding his body to her. Again and again she laid her face on his and wept for love and grief. Even death was overcome for a little while for here by the dead Osiris Isis conceived in her a son.

Next day she took a boat and carried the coffin back to Egypt. She never let it out of her sight again; except once after her hawk-headed son Horus had been born, when she went to visit him and left the coffin hidden in the marshes, and it so happened then that the wicked Set rode hunting there. He recognised it at once, who had set its timbers, hammered in its brass nails. He tore it open and rent Osiris' body limb from limb and scattered it widely in fourteen pieces, into the river, across the marsh. So Isis found on her return. Yet this time she did not weep. Patiently, silently, once again she sought her husband's body. Horus came to help her, her dog-headed nephew Anubis too, with her sister Nephys, wife of the wicked Set, and the moon-god Thoth, whose head was an ibis. Between them they found every piece, all except his penis which a fish had eaten in the river Nile. Isis took the rest and anointed them lovingly. Then she fitted them together one by one, and when his body was complete she swathed it in bandages and fanned it with her swallow's wings, singing her mourning song once more; my bed is lonely, my love, she sang, you do not see how our garden grows. But that was the end of it and afterwards she ceased to mourn – for in her making Osiris rose and was alive again. But he did not live with men, now he was an immortal god dwelling with the dead in the other world. Indeed he presides over them in judgement for eternity, weighing each man's heart in turn against a feather.

EGYPTIAN

Food Plants 117

Lament for Tammuz, the Harvest God

Her lament is the lament for a herb that grows not in the bed,
Her lament is the lament for the corn that grows not in the ear.
Her lament is for a great river where no willows grow,
Her lament is for a field where corn and herbs grow not,
Her lament is for a pool where fishes grow not.
Her lament is for a thicket of reeds where no reeds grow.
Her lament is for woods where tamarisks grow not.
Her lament is for a wilderness where no cypresses grow.
Her lament is for the depth of a garden of trees, where honey and
    wine grow not.
Her lament is for meadows where no plants grow.
Her lament is for a palace where length of life grows not.

BABYLONIAN

THE END OF THE WORLD

But what shall be the end of the little holiness
Which still dwells in my sand . . . ?
. . . Spring upright again, says the child,
To where tears mean eternity.

Nelly Sachs

Time will come, when days will be
sweet as nights
and beautiful for people
to whom time will be unimportant.

Then we shall know.

Yehuda Amichai

If the world had a beginning it might also, presumably, one day, come to an end. That is the logical conclusion. Yet not all mythologies make the jump from one to the other – for it is a jump. Maybe it's surprising rather how many do. Even then, having made it, the primitive mythologies think of it in the main in wholly practical terms; the props, legs, creatures that hold the world up or together, break or are broken or move away in the manner of props, legs, creatures. The more sophisticated mythologies on the other hand begin to impose the mythological pattern, and as Christians with the second coming or Jews with the advent of the Messiah, see it not only as an end but as a new beginning. In each case the world destruction is followed by a new age – a slate wiped clean, a new leaf turned – just as in the flood stories, to which these stories are often very close. The difference is that while the flood is history, the past, the end of the world stories are prophecy, the future. (That is, in most cases; in some, as in the story of Yima, though I place it here, it is not wholly certain which it is, past or future, history or prophecy.)

In other cases still the past and the future are directly linked, the mythologies concerned seeing the history of earth and mankind as an ongoing process of destruction and recreation. Thus the flood which once destroyed and recreated the world is merely an image of what is to come again, and maybe again and again and again. One version, the Hindu, sees that process as infinite, never-ending. Others, the Mayan and Aztec in particular, set a limit to the number of cycles – in fact see ourselves as confronting the very last cycle of all, and do not know what may replace it, if anything.

Yet what the primitive and more complex myths often have in common is the idea that actions of mankind can influence the event. They see the world as coming to an end – or entering a new phase of destruction – at least partly as a result of human behaviour. 'That day will be brought about by us, we men,' says the African story from the Fang people; the age will destroy us – 'if we let it, if we cease to redeem ourselves by work and sacrifice,' says the Aztec prophecy. Which is not to say that destruction is not felt to be inevitable in the end, even so, yet such pronouncements must seem to order a little that vastness in which man seems often so puny and helpless. If he but screams into it: 'Not only can I make myself a world, I can destroy it.

The End of the World   121

*I am truly the king of this castle,' for a while he is able to feel himself
that, precisely. He also appears, in the process, to enjoy himself hugely,
judging by the gusto of his accounts of it; first of the mighty disaster,
flood or fire or earthquake, dragon or tiger, blinding winter, burning
summer; thereafter of the eternal and beautiful future that succeeds
the disaster – which may be the physically described paradise of, say,
the Book of Revelations, the pure river, the universal tree, the no
need for sun or candle; or may be that less tangible, more mystical
peace, enfolded back into the mind of the one god, the Brahma, as in
the passage from the Indian epic, 'The Mahabharata'.*

*Incidentally, if you take that last passage, placing the origins of both
ourselves and our world firmly in the mind of the god, and if you set it
beside the statements from those modern physicists who see some kind
of intellect at work behind the universe, you may perhaps find yourself
shivering a little, not least at its immensity. As the Fang story concludes,
'I do not know, my brothers.' Oh how we do not know. . . .*

¶All moons, all years, all days, all winds, reach their completion
and pass away. So does all blood reach its place of quiet, as it
reaches its power and its throne. Measured was the time in which
they could praise the splendour of the trinity. Measured was the
time in which they could know the sun's benevolence. Measured was
the time in which the grid of the stars would look down upon them;
and through it, keeping watch over their safety, the gods trapped
within the stars would contemplate them.

CENTRAL AMERICA *Maya*

¶ Then Gangleri said: 'What is there to relate about Ragnarök?
I have never heard tell of this before.'

High One said: 'There are many and great tidings to tell about it.
First will come the winter called Fimbulvetr. Snow will drive from

all quarters, there will be hard frosts and biting winds; the sun will be no use. There will be three such winters on end with no summer between. Before that, however, three other winters will pass accompanied by great wars throughout the whole world. Brothers will kill each other for the sake of gain, and no one will spare father or son in manslaughter or in incest. As it says in the *Sibyl's Vision*:

> Brothers will fight
> and kill each other,
> siblings
> do incest;
> men will know misery,
> adulteries be multiplied,
> an axe-age, a sword-age,
> shields will be cloven,
> a wind-age, a wolf-age,
> before the world's ruin.

'Then will occur what will seem a great piece of news, the wolf will swallow the sun and that will seem a great disaster to men. Then another wolf will seize the moon and that one too will do great harm. The stars will disappear from heaven. Then this will come to pass, the whole surface of the earth and the mountains will tremble so violently that trees will be uprooted from the ground, mountains will crash down, and all fetters and bonds will be snapped and severed. The wolf Fenrir will get loose then. The sea will lash against the land because the Midgard Serpent is writhing in giant fury trying to come ashore. At that time, too, the ship known as Naglfar will become free. It is made of dead men's nails, so it is worth warning you that, if anyone dies with his nails uncut, he will greatly increase the material for that ship which both gods and men devoutly hope will take a long time building. In this tidal wave, however, Naglfar will be launched. The name of the giant steering Naglfar is Hrym. The wolf Fenrir will advance with wide open mouth, his upper jaw against the sky, his lower on the earth (he would gape more widely still if there were room) and his eyes and nostrils will blaze with fire. The Midgard Serpent will blow so much poison that the whole sky and sea will be spattered with it; he is most terrible and will be on the other side of the wolf.

The End of the World 123

'In this din the sky will be rent asunder and the sons of Muspell ride forth from it. Surt will ride first and with him fire blazing both before and behind. He has a very good sword and it shines more brightly than the sun. When they ride over Bifröst, however – as has been said before – that bridge will break. The sons of Muspell will push forward to the plain called Vígríd and the wolf Fenrir and the Midgard Serpent will go there too. Loki and Hrym with all the frost giants will also be there by then, and all the family of Hel will accompany Loki. The sons of Muspell, however, will form a host in themselves and that a very bright one. The plain Vígríd is a hundred and twenty leagues in every direction.

'When these things are happening, Heimdall will stand up and blow a great blast on the horn Gjöll and awaken all the gods and they will hold an assembly. Then Ódin will ride to Mímir's spring and ask Mímir's advice for himself and his company. The ash Yggdrasil will tremble and nothing in heaven or earth will be free from fear. The Æsir and all the Einherjar will arm themselves and press forward on the plain. Ódin will ride first in a helmet of gold and a beautiful coat of mail and with his spear Gungnir, and he will make for the wolf Fenrir. Thór will advance at his side but will be unable to help him, because he will have his hands full fighting the Midgard Serpent. Frey will fight against Surt and it will be a hard conflict before Frey falls; the loss of the good sword that he gave to Skírnir will bring about his death. Then the hound Garm, which was bound in front of Gnipahellir, will also get free; he is the worst sort of monster. He will battle with Týr and each will kill the other. Thór will slay the Midgard Serpent but stagger back only nine paces before he falls down dead, on account of the poison blown on him by the serpent. The wolf will swallow Ódin and that will be his death. Immediately afterwards, however, Vídar will stride forward and place one foot on the lower jaw of the wolf. On this foot he will be wearing the shoe which has been in the making since the beginning of time; it consists of the strips of leather men pare off at the toes and heels of their shoes, and for this reason people who want to help the Æsir must throw away these strips. Vídar will take the wolf's upper jaw in one hand and tear his throat asunder and that will be the wolf's death. Loki will battle with Heimdall and each will kill the other. Thereupon Surt will fling fire over the earth and burn up the whole word. As it says in the *Sibyl's Vision*:

> The sun will go black
> earth sink in the sea,
> heaven be stripped
> of its bright stars;
> smoke rage
> and fire,
> leaping the flame
> lick heaven itself.'

Then Gangleri asked: 'What will happen afterwards, when heaven and earth and the whole world has been burned and all the gods are dead and all the Einherjar and the whole race of man? Didn't you say before that everyone will go on living for ever in some world or other?'

Then Third answered: 'There will be many good dwelling-places then and many bad. The best place to be in at that time will be Gimlé in heaven, and for those that like it there is plenty of good drink in the hall called Brimir that is on Ókolnir. There is also an excellent hall on Nidafjöll called Sindri; it is made of red gold. Good and righteous men will live in these halls. On Nástrandir there is a large and horrible hall whose doors face north; it is made of the backs of serpents woven together like wattle-work, with all their heads turning in to the house and spewing poison so that rivers of it run through the hall. Perjurers and murderers wade these rivers. But it is worst of all in Hvergelmir.

> There Nidhogg bedevils
> the bodies of the dead.'

Then Gangleri asked: 'Will any of the gods be living then? Will there be any earth or heaven then?'

High One said: 'At that time earth will rise out of the sea and be green and fair, and fields of corn will grow that were never sown. Vídar and Váli will be living, so neither the sea nor Surt's Fire will have done them injury, and they will inhabit Idavöll where Ásgard used to be. And the sons of Thór, Módi and Magni will come there and possess Mjöllnir. After that Baldur and Höd will come from Hel. They will all sit down together and converse, calling to mind their hidden lore and talking about things that happened in the past, about the Midgard Serpent and the wolf Fenrir. Then they will find there in the grass the golden chessmen the Æsir used to own. While the world is being burned by Surt, in a place called Hoddmímir's Wood will be concealed two human beings called Líf and Lífthrasir. Their food will be the morning dews, and from these men will come so great a stock that the whole world will be peopled. And you will think this strange, but the sun will have borne a daughter no less lovely than herself, and she will follow the paths of her mother. And now, if you have anything more to ask, I can't think how you can manage it, for I've never heard anyone tell more of the story of the world. Make what use of it you can.'

ICELAND

The Disaster! What is the Disaster?
Would that you knew what the Disaster is!
On that day men shall become scattered moths
and the mountains like tufts of carded wool.
Then he whose scales are heavy shall dwell in bliss; but
he whose scales are light, the Abyss shall be his home.
Would that you knew what this is like!
It is a scorching fire.

MOSLEM The Koran

¶ Each age must come to an end at last. At the beginning of each the world is created and peopled – and just as each world before has grown evil in the end and been destroyed, so ours will be. The rain serpent reaching across the sky will belch forth torrents of water, and great streams too gush from the sun and moon. The old goddess waits, with her tiger claws; the crossbones, emblem of death, decorates her skirt and a crown of live snakes writhes upon her head; she halts the water for a while but not for long, because the

black god steps out, ready to destroy us all and on his fearsome head
an owl screeches in fury.

CENTRAL AMERICA Maya

... and the sun shall suddenly shine forth at night and
the moon during the day.
Blood shall drip from wood
And the stone shall utter its voice;
the peoples shall be troubled
And the stars shall fall.

JEWISH The Apocrypha

¶ In time to come the lakes will melt the foundations of the world
and the rivers will cut the world loose. Then it will float and that
will be the end of the world.

NORTH AMERICA Okanaga

¶ Finally Sinaa showed the Javuna visitor an enormous forked stick
that supported the sky and said, 'The day our people die out entirely,
I will pull this down, and the sky will collapse, and all people will
disappear. That will be the end of everything.'

SOUTH AMERICA, BRAZIL Xingu

... moreover; I shall destroy all that I have made.
The earth will be earth no longer but a deep abyss,
a flood in its primeval chaos,
And I the one remaining together with Osiris. ...

EGYPTIAN

¶ It will come to pass that a stupor will seize the people of the earth and they shall fall into many tribulations and when they abandon hope at last, the time of the Messiah shall awake. Into twelve parts is that time divided. In the first part there will be the beginning of commotions, and in the second there will be the slayings of the great ones. And in the third part the fall of many by death. And in the fourth the sending of desolation, in the fifth famine and the withholding of rain, in the sixth earthquakes and terrors, in the seventh many portents, in the eighth incursions of the shedim, in the ninth the fall of fire, in the tenth rapine and much oppression, in the eleventh wickedness and unchastity, in the twelfth confusions from the mingling together of all these things. They will belong to the whole earth but I will protect only those found in the land of Israel. And it will come to pass that when all is accomplished the Messiah will be revealed. And Behemoth will be revealed from his place and Leviathan will arise from the sea, those two great monsters which I created on the fifth day of creation and I kept them until that time. I will summon the angels at first to fight Leviathan but at one glance from him they shall flee in dismay from the battlefield, and I will order Leviathan and Behemoth to enter into battle with each other, and there Behemoth will drop dead from a blow of Leviathan's fin, and Leviathan will be killed by the lash of Behemoth's tail. And from the skin of Leviathan I will make tabernacles to shelter the righteous while they eat dishes made of his flesh. For the less worthy I will have coverings made, for the less worthy still necklaces, and for the least amulets, and all the rest of the skin will I spread above the walls of Jerusalem and its splendour will shine from one end of the earth to the other. The earth will reveal its fruit ten thousand fold and on one vine there will be a thousand branches, and each branch will produce a thousand clusters and each cluster will produce a thousand grapes and each grape will produce a cor of wine. And those who are hungry will rejoice. Moreover they will see marvels every day. And it will come to pass in those days when all has been fulfilled that the Messiah will return in glory and all those who have fallen asleep in hope of him will rise again from the dead.

JEWISH

¶ There were four suns before our own, and each in turn were destroyed and the whole world with them and all the men in the world. At the end of the first men were devoured by tigers. At the end of the second they were swept away by huge winds and those that were left changed into monkeys. At the end of the third came a rain of fire from the sky and burnt up everything and everyone; except only a few men and they turned into birds. Then came the fourth sun. This was the sun of the four waters, because when its turn came for destruction it was destroyed by flood and men were changed to fishes.

Now we live in the age of the fifth sun, which is our own, the sun of the centre, the sun of earthquakes, which will destroy us in the end; if we let it – if we cease to try to redeem ourselves by work and sacrifice.

CENTRAL AMERICA *Aztec*

¶ When the great god Ulgen sends Maidere down to earth to teach the people and convert them to his worship, the evil Elrik will stand against him jealously and threaten Maidere with a raised sword. But Maidere will not retreat; so then Elrik will kill him, and his blood will turn the whole world red, then set itself on fire and the flames will reach as high as heaven. Ulgen will clap his hand seeing them and call on the dead to rise at once, from beneath the sea, from the depths of the mountain, from the hidden places of the forests; wherever it was that death came upon them. But when the world burns Elrik will burn too and with him all the wicked who followed him.

RUSSIA *Altai Tartars*

¶ Oh beauteous Yima: on the evil material world the evil winters are about to fall; that shall bring the fierce deadly frosts, while the snowflakes fall thickly on the highest mountains, in the deepest valleys. And the beasts that live in the desert and the beasts that live

The End of the World 129

on the tops of the mountains and the beasts that live safely in the valleys will all take shelter. And where before those winters grew rich grass for cattle, when the snows melt people will marvel to find the footprint of a single sheep.

Therefore, Yima, make an enclosure as long as a riding-ground on every side of the square, and bring there the seeds of oxen, men and sheep, of dogs, of birds, of red blazing fires. Make water flow there and make the birds settle on green that never fades and give them food that never fails. Make houses each with a balcony, a courtyard and a gallery.

Bring the seeds of men and women, the greatest and the best and the finest upon earth. Bring the seeds of every kind of tree, the highest and sweetest-smelling; of fruit, the finest-tasting, the sweetest-smelling. Bring two of every kind and keep them there as long as men must stay in the enclosure.

There shall be no hump-backed there or pigeon-chested, no leper, no lunatic, no birthmark or pockmark, none deformed of teeth or mind or limb, no liar, no bearer of malice, no one jealous or spiteful.

Make nine streets in the largest part of your enclosure, Yima, six in the middle part, three in the smallest. To the largest bring a thousand seeds of men and women, to the middle six hundred, to the smallest three hundred. Then seal up your enclosure with your golden seal and make a door in it and a window self-shining within.

Yima said: How shall I make this enclosure you have commanded me to make?

Oh beauteous Yima. Stamp your feet and crush the earth. Then knead it with your hands as a potter kneads the clay.

So Yima made it. Men lead a good life within the enclosure that he made, kneading the earth with his hands as a potter kneads the clay. And when the winters descend on the evil material world, when the deadly frosts freeze it, and the snows cover it up, they will still live safely there until all hundred evil winters have passed away. Then Yima will replenish the earth with flocks of sheep and herds of oxen, with men and dogs and birds and red blazing fires, until there will be no more room for flocks or herds or men.

PERSIAN

¶ Listen how Brahma who is eternal and undecaying, without beginning and without end, repeatedly creates and destroys all created objects. When his day expires and night comes he longs for sleep, and at such a time he urges the being called Maharadh, one conscious of great powers, who having assembled himself in the form of hundreds and thousands of rays, is then divided into a dozen portions each resembling a blazing fire, and so consumes with his energy the four kinds of created being. All mobile and immobile creatures thus destroyed within the twinkling of an eye, the earth is left as bare as a tortoise shell. Then Rudra of immeasurable sight first swiftly overwhelms the earth with water, then creates the Yuga fire which dries up that water. Then comes the mighty wind, immeasurably powerful in his eight forms. Having swallowed up that blazing fire with its seven flames, he courses in all directions, upwards, downwards, across every part. Then an immeasurable space swallows up that transcendent wind, then the mind cheerfully swallows up the immeasurable space, then consciousness, the Lord of all creatures, swallows up the mind and is in turn swallowed by the soul that knows past, present and future; which soul or universe is swallowed at the last by Brahma, Lord of all things. His hands and feet extend over every part. His eyes and head and face are everywhere, his ears reach every place, he overwhelms all things. He is the heart of all things, he is the measure of a digit of a thumb. That infinite and supreme soul, that utter Lord, he swallows up the universe and falls asleep at last.

INDIA

¶ The tribe listens silently. Only one man speaks.

In the beginning sun and moon were man and wife. The moon bore the sun many children and they were called the stars. This family did not eat food of the kind we eat, it nourished itself on fire, and so the whole family shone and gave light to us on earth. In the beginning sun and moon were man and wife. The stars were their children.

The End of the World   131

And then one day there came to the village a young man so handsome that the moon's heart was instantly enflamed by love. She gave him a token and said, wait for me at the bend in the road and I will fly away with you for ever.

Where is she? the sun asked his children the stars when he noticed the moon's absence. They did not know. Where is she? – I ask you. But now he shone so angrily the stars ran away from him. You must have helped her flee, he said and began to hunt them down. Every time he caught a star he devoured it, and that star shone no more. But the rest were too scattered and numerous for him to catch and eat them all.

And so each day still the sun chases moon and stars across the sky. Sometimes he eats another of the stars; the moon, good mother that she is, tries to protect her children, warning them of the sun's rising and taking them with her to her hiding place.

This chase will last a long time. But it must come to an end some day. And that day will be brought about by us, us men. It is for us to uphold the rule of good on earth. If we do not then evil will reign instead. And on the day that evil reigns the sun will capture his wife at last, but this time he will not devour her. The sun will lock the moon in a deep ditch at the centre of the earth and he will never let her rise again. As for the stars, her children; their father, the sun, will soon catch and eat them, every one.

'And what will be our fate?' asks the tribe.

The speaker sighs. 'Who knows? Who knows? I do not know, my brothers.'

WEST AFRICA, GABON *Fang*

¶ And I saw a new heaven, and a new earth: for the first heaven, and the first earth were passed away, and there was no more sea.

And I heard a great voice out of heaven, saying, Behold, the tabernacle of God is with men, and he will dwell with them, and they shall be his people, and God himself shall be with them, and be their God.

And God shall wipe away all tears from their eyes: and there shall be no more death, neither sorrow, nor crying, neither shall there be any more pain: for the former things are passed away.

And he that sat upon the throne said unto me, It is done: I am Alpha and Omega, the beginning and the end. I will give unto him that is athirst, of the fountain of the water of life, freely.

He that overcometh, shall inherit all things, and I will be his God, and he shall be my son.

But the fearful, and the unbelieving, and the abominable, and murderers, and whoremongers, and sorcerers, and idolaters, and all liars, shall have their part in the lake which burneth with fire and brimstone: which is the second death.

And there came unto me one of the seven Angels, which had the seven vials full of the seven last plagues, and talked with me, saying, Come hither, I will shew thee the Bride, the Lamb's wife.

And he carried me away in the spirit to a great and high mountain, and shewed me that great city, the holy Jerusalem, descending out of heaven from God,

Having the glory of God: and her light was like unto a stone most precious, even like a jasper stone, clear as crystal,

And had a wall, great and high, and had twelve gates, and at the gates twelve Angels, and names written thereon, which are the names of the twelve tribes of the children of Israel:

And the building of the wall of it was of jasper, and the city was pure gold, like unto clear glass.

And the foundations of the wall of the city were garnished with all manner of precious stones. The first foundation was jasper, the second sapphire, the third a chalcedony, the fourth an emerald,

The fifth sardonyx, the sixth sardius, the seventh chrysolite, the eighth beryl, the ninth a topaz, the tenth a chrysoprasus, the eleventh a jacinth, the twelfth an amethyst.

And the twelve gates were twelve pearls, every several gates was of one pearl, and the street of the city was pure gold, as it were transparent glass.

And I saw no temple therein: for the Lord God Almighty, and the Lamb, are the temple of it.

And he shewed me a pure river of water of life, clear as crystal, proceeding out of the throne of God, and of the Lamb.

The End of the World 133

And in the midst of the street of it, and on either side of the river, was there the tree of life, which bore twelve manner of fruits, and yielded her fruit every month: and the leaves of the tree were for the healing of the nations.

And there shall be no more curse, but the throne of God, and of the Lamb shall be in it, and his servants shall serve him;

And they shall see his face, and his name shall be in their foreheads.

And there shall be no night there, and they need no candle, neither light of the sun, for the Lord God giveth them light, and they shall reign for ever and ever.

THE NEW TESTAMENT: *The Revelation of St John*
21: 1, 3, 4, 6–12, 18–22
22: 1–5

In the process of assembling material for this collection it became clear to me that the best course would be to leave the stories as far as possible alone; too many interpolations, additions or rearrangements being all too likely to distort the point and purpose of the originals besides depriving them to some extent of their local particularity. This is especially true of the more primitive stories, often presented in the barest outline; quite deliberately in many cases I have preserved this bareness, though extending the story where necessary to make a more coherent narrative; and even this I felt sometimes might be going too far. Elsewhere of course there are stories which have emerged from elaborate literary traditions, and here, if I haven't used a direct translation I have tried in my retelling to give a sense of that tradition. I have also sometimes assembled one story from many versions – as with the chameleon story of the origin of death which appears in many parts of Africa. Only in one or two instances have I taken a myth and though retaining the basic story-line added to it somewhat. The flood story from Siberia is the chief example. All I had originally was a handful of sentences – but since the hero, Noj, obviously derived from Noah himself I saw no reason why I too shouldn't embroider the idea a little, much as mediaeval mystery plays embroidered the Biblical myths. It gave me some amusement certainly. Otherwise let the stories speak for themselves. They are much too good to need any further help from me.

Earth

page

8 *Central America, Maya :* reprinted from *The Book of Chilam Balam,* translated by Irene Nicholson, MEXICAN AND CENTRAL AMERICAN MYTHOLOGY, The Hamlyn Publishing Group Ltd., Feltham, Middlesex.

8 *Africa, Tanzania, Wapangwa :* reprinted from THE ORIGINS OF LIFE AND DEATH edited by Ulli Beier, Heinemann Educational Books Ltd., London.

8 *Hawaii :* reprinted from THE KUMULIPO translated by Martha Warren Beckwith, University of Chicago Press, Chicago.

9 *India, Hill Miri :* reprinted from MYTHS OF THE NORTHEAST FRONTIER collected by Verrier Elwin, North East Frontier Agency, Arunachal Pradesh, India.

10 *Bulgaria :* adapted from FINNO-UGRIC, SIBERIAN MYTHOLOGY edited by Uno Holmberg (The Mythology of All Races series, vol. IV, series editor: John A. MacCulloch), Cooper Square Publishers, Inc., New York, 1927.

13 *Africa, Dahomey :* adapted from THE DAHOMEY by M. J. Herskovitz, J. J. Augustin, Inc., Locust Valley, New York.

15 *India, Baiga :* reprinted from MYTHS OF MIDDLE INDIA collected by Verrier Elwin, Oxford University Press, Bombay.

18 *North America, Chuhwuht :* reprinted from THE INDIANS' BOOK by Natalie Curtis, Dover Publications, Inc., New York.

19 *India, Hrusso :* reprinted from MYTHS OF THE NORTHEAST FRONTIER collected by Verrier Elwin, North East Frontier Agency, Arunachal Pradesh, India.

20 *Finland :* adapted from *The Kalevala.*

22 *New Zealand, Maori :* adapted from NEW ZEALAND AND ITS INHABITANTS by R. Taylor.

22 *India, Rori :* reprinted from MYTHS OF THE NORTHEAST FRONTIER collected by Verrier Elwin, North East Frontier Agency, Arunachal Pradesh, India.

Man

26 *Africa, Kenya, Nandi :* reprinted from THE NANDI: THEIR LANGUAGE AND FOLKLORE by A. C. Hollis, edited by G. W. B. Huntingford, Clarendon Press, Oxford, 1909.

28 *Russia :* adapted from FINNO-UGRIC, SIBERIAN MYTHOLOGY edited by Uno Holmberg (The Mythology of All Races series, vol. IV, series editor:

John A. MacCulloch), Cooper Square Publishers, Inc., New York, 1927.

28 *South America, Brazil, Xingu:* reprinted from XINGU: THE INDIANS, THEIR MYTHS by Orlando and Claudio Villas Boas, Farrar, Straus & Giroux, Inc., New York; Souvenir Press Ltd., London.

28 *Australia, Queensland:* adapted from OCEANIC MYTHOLOGY edited by Roland B. Dixon (The Mythology of All Races series, vol. IX, series editor: John A. MacCulloch), Cooper Square Publishers, Inc., New York, 1927.

29 *India, Hindi:* reprinted from HINDU MYTHS translated by Wendy Doniger O'Flaherty, Penguin Classics 1975, page 28 Penguin Books Ltd., Harmondsworth, Middlesex.

29 *Russia, Altai Tartar:* adapted from FINNO-UGRIC, SIBERIAN MYTHOLOGY edited by Uno Holmberg (The Mythology of All Races series, vol. IV, series editor: John A. MacCulloch), Cooper Square Publishers, Inc., New York, 1927.

30 *Central America, Maya:* adapted from *The Popul Vuh.*

31 *North Borneo, Dusuns:* reprinted from THE RELIGION OF THE TEMPASHK DUSUNS OF NORTH BORNEO by H. N. Evans, Cambridge University Press Ltd., London.

31 *New Zealand, Maori:* adapted from OCEANIC MYTHOLOGY edited by Roland B. Dixon (The Mythology of All Races series, vol. IX, series editor: John A. MacCulloch), Cooper Square Publishers, Inc., New York, 1927.

32 *Russia, Bashkir:* reprinted from SIBERIAN MYTHOLOGY by C. Fillingham Coxwell, The C. W. Daniel Co. Ltd., London.

35 *North Borneo, Kyan:* adapted from OCEANIC MYTHOLOGY edited by Roland B. Dixon (The Mythology of All Races series, vol. IX, series editor: John A. MacCulloch), Cooper Square Publishers, Inc., New York, 1927.

35 *India, Kol:* reprinted from MYTHS OF MIDDLE INDIA, collected by Verrier Elwin, Oxford University Press, Bombay.

35 *Moslem:* reprinted from THE KORAN translated by N. J. Dawood, Penguin Classics 1974 (fourth edition), page 220, Penguin Books Ltd., Harmondsworth, Middlesex.

36 *Melanesia, New Hebrides:* adapted from OCEANIC MYTHOLOGY edited by Roland B. Dixon (The Mythology of All Races series, vol. IX, series editor: John A. MacCulloch), Cooper Square Publishers, Inc., New York 1927.

37 *North America, Mandan:* adapted from NORTH AMERICAN INDIAN MYTHOLOGY, edited by Cottie Burland, The Hamlyn Group Ltd., Feltham, Middlesex.

37 *Africa, Gabon, Fang:* originally published in ANTHOLOGIE NEGRE edited by Blaise Cendrars, Editions Buchet-Chastel, Paris; reprinted from

THE ORIGINS OF LIFE AND DEATH edited by Ulli Beier, Heinemann Educational Books Ltd., London.

40   *Indo-China, Wa :* adapted from INDO-CHINESE MYTHOLOGY edited by Sir James Scott (The Mythology of All Races series, vol. XII, series editor: John A. MacCulloch), Cooper Square Publishers, Inc., New York, 1927.

Flood

46   *North America, Inuit :* reprinted from THE CENTRAL ESKIMO by Franz Boas, *Sixth Annual Report of the Bureau of Ethnology*, Government Printing Office, Washington, D.C., 1888.

46   *Babylonian :* reprinted from THE EPIC OF GILGAMESH translated by N. K. Sandars, Penguin Classics (1974 reprint), pages 108–113, Penguin Books Ltd., Harmondsworth, Middlesex.

50   *India, Bhil :* reprinted from MYTHS OF MIDDLE INDIA collected by Verrier Elwin, Oxford University Press, Bombay.

51   *Indonesia, Nias :* adapted from OCEANIC MYTHOLOGY edited by Roland B. Dixon (The Mythology of All Races series, vol. IX, series editor: John A. MacCulloch), Cooper Square Publishers, Inc., New York, 1927.

52   *North America, Mojave Apache :* reprinted from THE INDIANS' BOOK by Natalie Curtis, Dover Publications, Inc., New York.

54   *Melanesia, Caroline Islands :* adapted from OCEANIC MYTHOLOGY edited by Roland B. Dixon (The Mythology of All Races series, vol. IX, series editor: John A. MacCulloch), Cooper Square Publishers, Inc., New York, 1927.

55   *Australia, Victoria :* adapted from OCEANIC MYTHOLOGY edited by Roland B. Dixon (The Mythology of All Races series, vol. IX, series editor: John A. MacCulloch), Cooper Square Publishers, Inc., New York, 1927.

55   *New Guinea, Papua :* adapted from PAPUAN FAIRY TALES by Annie Ker, London, 1850.

56   *Ireland :* reprinted from CELTIC MISCELLANY translated by Kenneth Hurlstone Jackson, Routledge & Kegan Paul Ltd., London.

57   *Chinese :* adapted from *The Chu Ching.*

58   *South America, Sherente :* adapted from THE RAW AND THE COOKED: *Introduction to a Science of Mythology* by Claude Lévi-Strauss, Jonathan Cape Ltd., London; Harper & Row, Inc., New York.

59   *Russia, Siberia :* adapted from FINNO-UGRIC, SIBERIAN MYTHOLOGY edited by Uno Holmberg (The Mythology of All Races series, vol. IV, series editor: John A. MacCulloch), Cooper Square Publishers, Inc., New York, 1927.

Fire

66   *Thailand :* adapted from MYTHS OF THE ORIGINS OF FIRE by Sir James Frazer, The Macmillan Co. Ltd., London.

68 *Russia, Siberia:* adapted from SIBERIAN MYTHOLOGY by C. Fillingham Coxwell, The C. W. Daniel Co. Ltd., London.

69 *Africa:* adapted from AFRICAN MYTHOLOGY by Geoffrey Parrinder (World Mythology series), Leon Amiel Publishers, New York.

70 *North America:* adapted from MYTHS OF THE ORIGINS OF FIRE by Sir James Frazer, The Macmillan Co. Ltd., London, 1930.

72 *Finland:* adapted from *The Kalevala.*

72 *New Zealand, Maori:* reprinted from POLYNESIAN MYTHOLOGY by Sir George Gray.

75 *South America, Kayape Gorotive:* adapted from THE RAW AND THE COOKED: *Introduction to a Science of Mythology* by Claude Lévi-Strauss, Jonathan Cape Ltd., London; Harper & Row Inc., New York.

77 *India:* reprinted from MYTHS OF MIDDLE INDIA collected by Verrier Elwin, Oxford University Press, Bombay.

77 *Greek:* adaptation of 'Prometheus' by Penelope Farmer.

Death

84 *Greek:* adaptation of 'Pandora' by Judith Vidal Hall.

90 *South America, Peru:* adapted from LAROUSSE WORLD MYTHOLOGY translated by P. Beardsworth, The Hamlyn Group, Feltham, Middlesex; G. P. Putnam's Sons, New York.

91 *Chinese:* adapted from SONGS AND STORIES OF THE CH'UAN MIAO translated by D. C. Graham from *Smithsonian Miscellaneous Collections,* Chapter 1, Volume 123, Smithsonian Institution Press, Washington, D.C.

93 *Japanese:* adapted from *The Kojiki.*

96 *North America, Navaho:* adapted from NORTH AMERICAN INDIAN MYTHOLOGY edited by Cottie Burland, The Hamlyn Group Ltd., Feltham, Middlesex.

98 *India, Hindi:* adapted from *The Mahabharata.*

101 *Africa, Nigeria, Nupe:* reprinted from THE ORIGINS OF LIFE AND DEATH edited by Ulli Beier, Heinemann Educational Books Ltd., London.

Food Plants

106 *Finland, Mordvin:* reprinted from FINNO-UGRIC, SIBERIAN MYTHO-LOGY edited by Uno Holmberg (The Mythology of All Races series, vol. IV, series editor: John A. MacCulloch), Cooper Square Publishers, Inc., New York, 1927.

107 *Madagascar:* adapted from LAROUSSE WORLD MYTHOLOGY translated by P. Beardsworth, The Hamlyn Group Ltd., Feltham, Middlesex; G. P. Putnam's Sons, New York.

108 *Russia, Siberia:* adapted from SIBERIAN MYTHOLOGY by C. Filling-ham Coxwell, The C. W. Daniel Co. Ltd., London.

111 *North America, Canada:* reprinted from CANADIAN WONDER TALES by Cyrus Macmillan, The Bodley Head Ltd., London.

113 *New Guinea, West Ceram:* translated by Penelope Farmer from Janson's RELIGIOUSE WELDBILD FRUHER CULTUR, August Schröder Verlag.

118 *Babylonian:* reprinted from THE GOLDEN BOUGH translated by Sir James Frazer, The Macmillan Co. Ltd., London.

The End of the World

122 *Central America, Maya:* reprinted from MEXICAN AND CENTRAL AMERICAN MYTHOLOGY translated by Irene Nicholson, The Hamlyn Group Ltd., Feltham, Middlesex.

122 *Iceland:* reprinted from SNORRI STURLUSON, THE PROSE EDDA, TALES FROM NORSE MYTHOLOGY translated by Jean I. Young, The Bodley Head Ltd., London.

126 *Moslem:* reprinted from THE KORAN translated by N. J. Dawood, Penguin Classics 1974 (fourth edition), page 29, Penguin Books Ltd., Harmondsworth, Middlesex.

126 *Central America, Maya:* interpretation of 'The Dresden Codex' by Penelope Farmer.

127 *North America, Okanaga:* reprinted from INDIAN LEGENDS OF THE NORTHWEST PACIFIC collected by Ella E. Clark, University of California Press, Berkeley, California.

127 *South America, Brazil, Xingu:* reprinted from XINGU: THE INDIANS, THEIR MYTHS by Claudio and Orlando Villas Boas, Farrar, Straus & Giroux, Inc., New York; Souvenir Press Ltd., London.

131 *India:* adapted from *The Mahabharata.*

131 *West Africa, Gabon, Fang:* translated and adapted by Penelope Farmer from AFRIKANISCHE LEGENDEN by Carl Einstein, Rowohlt Taschenbuch Verlag, Berlin.

Some people may be interested enough to want to seek out further material on their own account. It is easily done, and it does not matter really where they start. The folklore and ethnology sections of any good library will do as a beginning. So it was for me in any case. It was thus that I came across Stith Thompson's MOTIF-INDEX OF FOLK LITERATURE (Indiana University Press, Bloomington and London, 1955); for all the themes he gives, whose source turns out to be some book or journal published in Lithuanian or Rumanian or some other language equally inaccessible to the average English reader, there are plenty much more easily located. And thus it was also that I found the thirteen-volume collection *The Mythology of All Races*, edited by John A. MacCulloch (Cooper Square Publishers, 1927). But if these seem too specialist and hard to find, then available almost anywhere are:

NEW LAROUSSE ENCYCLOPAEDIA OF MYTHOLOGY introduced by Robert Graves, edited by Felix Guirand, and LAROUSSE WORLD MYTHOLOGY edited by Pierre Grimal (The Hamlyn Publishing Group 1963 and 1965), both a rich source of themes from all over the world.

Also useful are the following:

THE MASKS OF GOD by Joseph Campbell (Souvenir Press, 1973, four vols.)

MIDDLE EASTERN MYTHOLOGY by S. H. Hooke (Penguin Books, 1978)

GODS AND MYTHS OF NORTHERN EUROPE by H. R. Ellis Davidson (Penguin Books, 1977)

TALES OF THE NORTH AMERICAN INDIANS selected and annotated by Stith Thompson (Indiana University Press: Midland Books, Bloomington and London, 1966)

Finally, all books quoted here as sources are mostly worth further investigation. In particular I recommend the collections, made by Verrier Elwin, of stories from various parts of the Indian sub-continent: marvellous material which happens to have found a superb collector whose work deserves to be known a good deal more widely than it is. Also to be recommended is a mythology series containing such titles as INDIAN MYTHOLOGY, AFRICAN MYTHOLOGY, JAPANESE MYTHOLOGY etc. (The Hamlyn Publishing Group) which is, alas, rapidly going out of print but certain volumes from which can still be found in some bookshops and most libraries; all are by different authors, and all very fully illustrated so that you can get a good idea of the artefacts arising from the mythology as well as the myths themselves.

The Editor and Publishers are indebted to the following for their kind permission to reprint the following copyright material included in this volume:
Faber & Faber Ltd., London, and Harcourt Brace Jovanovich, Inc., New York, for an excerpt from 'East Coker' in FOUR QUARTETS by T. S. Eliot, copyright 1943 by T. S. Eliot, copyright 1971 by Esme Valerie Eliot, and an excerpt from 'The Journey of the Magi' in COLLECTED POEMS 1909-1962 by T. S. Eliot, copyright 1936 by Harcourt Brace Jovanovich, Inc., copyright © 1963, 1964 by T. S. Eliot; Little Brown & Co., Boston, for an excerpt from 'I Saw No Way' in THE COMPLETE POEMS OF EMILY DICKINSON, copyright 1935 by Martha Dickinson Bianchi, copyright © 1963 by Mary L. Hampson; The Hamlyn Publishing Group Ltd., Feltham, Middlesex, for extracts from MEXICAN AND CENTRAL AMERICAN MYTHOLOGY translated by Irene Nicholson, and NORTH AMERICAN INDIAN MYTHOLOGY edited by Cottie Burland; Heinemann Educational Books Ltd., London, and Editions Buchet-Chastel, Paris, for extracts from THE ORIGINS OF LIFE AND DEATH edited by Ulli Beier; University of Chicago Press, Chicago, for an extract from THE KUMULIPO translated by Martha Warren Beckwith; The North Eastern Frontier Agency, Arunachal Pradesh, India, for extracts from MYTHS OF THE NORTHEAST FRONTIER collected by Verrier Elwin; Mrs Lila Elwin for extracts from MYTHS OF MIDDLE INDIA collected by Verrier Elwin, published by Oxford University Press, Bombay; Dover Publications, Inc., New York, for extracts from THE INDIANS' BOOK by Natalie Curtis; Oxford University Press, Oxford, for extracts from THE NANDI: THEIR LANGUAGE AND FOLKLORE by A. C. Hollis, edited by G. W. B. Huntingford; Faber & Faber Ltd., London, and Harper & Row, Publishers, Inc., New York, for an excerpt from 'Examination at the Womb Door' in CROW by Ted Hughes; Farrar, Straus & Giroux, Inc., New York, and Souvenir Press Ltd., London, for extracts from XINGU: THE INDIANS, THEIR MYTHS by Orlando and Claudio Villas Boas, copyright © 1970 by Orlando and Claudio Villas Boas, this translation copyright © 1973 by Farrar, Straus & Giroux, Inc.; Penguin Books Ltd., Harmondsworth, Middlesex, for extracts from HINDU MYTHS translated by Wendy Doniger O'Flaherty, Copyright © by Wendy Doniger O'Flaherty, 1975, THE KORAN translated by N. J. Dawood, Copyright © N. J. Dawood, 1956, 1959, 1966, 1968, 1974, and THE EPIC OF GILGAMESH translated by N. K. Sandars, Copyright © N. K. Sandars, 1960, 1964, 1972; Cambridge University Press Ltd., London, for an extract from THE RELIGION OF THE TEMPASHK DUSUNS OF NORTH BORNEO by H. N. Evans; The C. W. Daniel Co. Ltd., London, for an extract from SIBERIAN MYTHOLOGY by C. Fillingham Coxwell; The Estate of the Late

Pablo Neruda, Jonathan Cape Ltd., London, and Farrar, Straus & Giroux, Inc., New York, for an excerpt from 'Daylight With Night Key' in EXTRA-VAGARIA by Pablo Neruda, translated by Alastair Reid, translation copyright © 1960, 1970, 1972, 1974 by Alastair Reid; Jonathan Cape Ltd., London, and E. P. Dutton & Co., Inc., New York, for an excerpt from THE WAY OF THE SUFI by Idries Shah; The Smithsonian Institution Press, Washington, D.C., for an extract from 'The Central Eskimo' by Frank Boas from THE SIXTH ANNUAL REPORT OF THE BUREAU OF ETHNOLOGY, Government Printing Office, Washington D.C.; Routledge & Kegan Paul Ltd., London, for an extract from CELTIC MISCELLANY translated by Kenneth Hurlstone Jackson; Judith Vidal Hall for the story 'Pandora', copyright © 1978 by Judith Vidal Hall; Cooper Square Publishers, Inc., New York, for an extract from FINNO-UGRIC, SIBERIAN MYTHOLOGY edited by Uno Holmberg (The Mythology of All Races series, vol. IV); The Bodley Head Ltd., London, for extracts from CANADIAN WONDER TALES by Cyrus Macmillan, and SNORRI STURLUSON, THE PROSE EDDA, TALES FROM NORSE MYTHOLOGY, translated by Jean I. Young and published by Bowes & Bowes; August Schröder Verlag for an extract from Janson's RELIGIOUSE WELDBILD FRUHER CULTUR; The Estate of the Late Sir James Frazer and A. P. Watt & Son, London, for 'Lament for Tammuz, The Harvest God' from THE GOLDEN BOUGH translated by Sir James Frazer, published by The Macmillan Co., London; Jonathan Cape Ltd., London, and Farrar, Straus & Giroux, Inc., New York, for an excerpt from 'The Voice of the Holy Land' in SELECTED POEMS/O THE CHIMNEYS by Nelly Sachs, translated by Ruth and Matthew Mead, copyright © 1967 by Farrar, Straus & Giroux, Inc.; Harper & Row, Publishers, Inc., New York, and Olwyn Hughes for an excerpt from 'We Were Near' in AMEN by Yehuda Amichai, translated by Ted Hughes, copyright © 1977 by Yehuda Amichai and Ted Hughes; University of California Press, Berkeley, California, for an extract from INDIAN LEGENDS OF THE NORTHWEST PACIFIC collected by Ella E. Clark, copyright © 1953 by The Regents of the University of California; The Estate of the Late Carl Einstein for extracts from AFRIKANISCHE LEGENDEN by Carl Einstein, published by Rowohlt Taschenbuch Verlag, Berlin.

The Editor also wishes to thank the following publishers for allowing her to adapt passages from works published by them as listed:

J. J. Augustin, Inc., New York: THE DAHOMEY by M. J. Herskovitz.

Cooper Square Publishers, Inc., New York: FINNO-UGRIC, SIBERIAN MYTHOLOGY edited by Uno Holmberg, OCEANIC MYTHOLOGY edited by Roland B. Dixon, INDO-CHINESE MYTHOLOGY edited by Sir James Scott (The Mythology of All Races series, series editor: John A. MacCulloch, vols. IV, IX, XII).

The Hamlyn Group Ltd., Feltham, Middlesex: NORTH AMERICAN INDIAN MYTHOLOGY edited by Cottie Burland.

The Hamlyn Group Ltd., Feltham, Middlesex, and G. P. Putnam's Sons, New York: LAROUSSE WORLD MYTHOLOGY edited by Pierre Grimal.

Jonathan Cape Ltd., London, and Harper & Row, Publishers, Inc., New York: THE RAW AND THE COOKED: Introduction to a Science of Mythology: by Claude Lévi-Strauss, translated by John and Doreen Weightman, copyright © 1964 by Librairie Plon, English translation copyright © 1969 by Harper & Row, Publishers, Inc., New York.

The Macmillan Co. Ltd., London: MYTHS OF THE ORIGIN OF FIRE by Sir James Frazer.

The C. W. Daniel Co. Ltd., London: SIBERIAN MYTHOLOGY by C. Fillingham Coxwell.

Leon Amiel Publishers, New York: AFRICAN MYTHOLOGY by Geoffrey Parrinder (World Mythology series).

Smithsonian Institution Press, New York: 'Songs and Stories of the Ch'uan Miao' translated by D. C. Graham, from SMITHSONIAN MISCELLANEOUS COLLECTIONS, Volume 123.